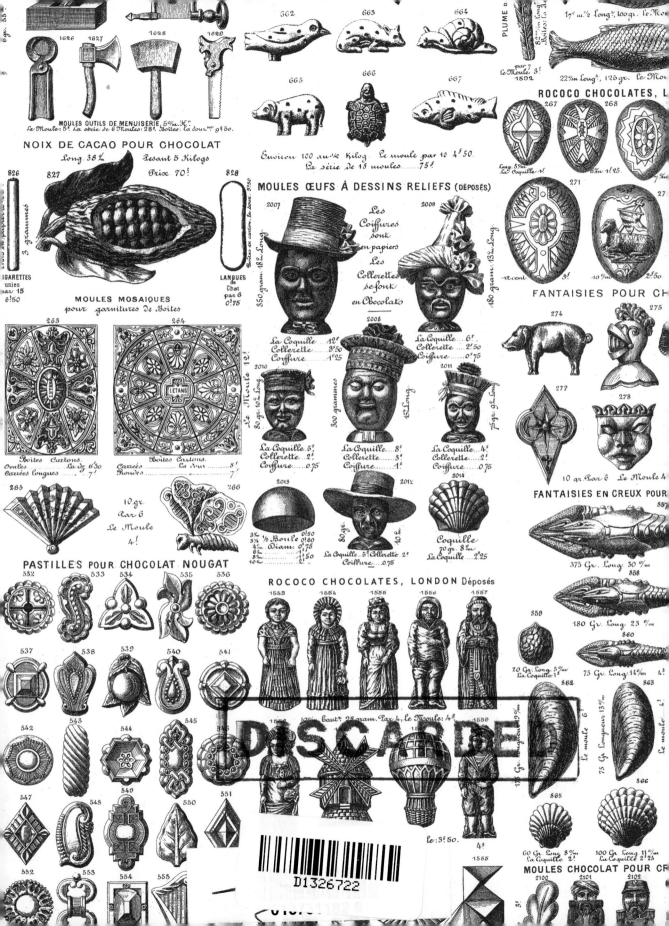

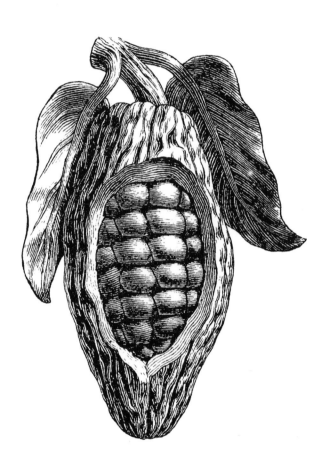

ROCOCO

MASTERING THE ART
OF CHOCOLATE

Chantal Coady

Weidenfeld & Nicolson
LONDON

This book is dedicated to the memory of chocolate activist, the late Doug Browne (1966–2008) whose gentle spirit still guides the Grenada Chocolate Company, and to Mott Green, Edmond Brown, Miss Joyce, Shadel Nyack-Compton and all the skilled farm crew who work the land and make some of the very finest chocolate in the world, sustainably and ethically.

They are a huge source of inspiration!

CONTENTS

INTRODUCTION

Writing this book has given me great pleasure. For me, chocolate is a deeply emotional subject. I am obsessed, and am fortunate enough to be surrounded by several tons of the best chocolate in the world.

EARLY ADVENTURES

I was born in Tehran and had a globetrotting childhood before moving to London. I recall, at the age of four, standing at the edge of a lily pond just outside Addis Ababa with my family. I had an overwhelming urge to walk on the lily pads, though I was fully clothed. As my feet settled on a lily pad, it sank and I was in the water. Much drama ensued as I was pulled out, and it took me years to admit to my mother that it was no accident; I had quite deliberately stepped in. This event was just one of many that came to symbolise my sense of adventure and desire to break the rules just to see what happens.

When I was six, my father secured the post of Senior Registrar at the Hospital for Tropical Diseases at St Pancras, London. We started the long journey to England on a merchant vessel called *The Zemoon*, by dint of my father being ship's doctor. We set off through the Gulf of Suez and then up the canal itself, shortly before it was closed by the long Arab-Israeli war, stopping at Piraeus for Easter Weekend. My birthday fell on Easter Sunday, and I recall a huge chocolate cake and thick creamy Greek yogurt; the first of many chocolate experiences that left an indelible impression on my mind.

At the hospital, all of Dr Coady's five children were expected to take part in the yearly ritual of a Christmas Day ward round. The huge excitement of receiving a big box of chocolates from the patients with a pretty picture on the front (some bucolic scene, no doubt) was swiftly extinguished when we discovered the contents were inedible and covered in a white bloom. It was clear they had vintage pedigree. Feelings of disappointment buried themselves deep in the recesses of my mind, and the seed was sown: I needed to create an idyllic chocolate experience.

The VW Beetle, our family car, in Addis Ababa: seven of us frequently travelled in it: my sister and I in the bucketseat, our two older siblings in the middle, our baby brother in his carry cot and our parents at the front. Photograph by Sybil Coady.

CONVENT SCHOOL: MY FIRST CHOCOLATE EXPERIMENT

We lived in Kuwait for a time and when I was nine I was despatched to a convent school in England, where my older sister was already installed. I was looking forward to joining her but the reality was a cold and stark one. The rambling buildings were freezing and the food practically inedible. The lack of warmth, banter and good food was somewhat compensated for by parcels from home containing our favourite things. The chocolate in these parcels was a comfort blanket in so many ways: it gave me a warm glow and a sense of security in my turbulent teenage years of incarceration at school, far away from home comforts.

I experimented with chocolate in my school holidays. On one ill-fated occasion I bought an egg mould, melted some Cadbury's Dairy Milk chocolate, poured the melted chocolate into the mould and put it in the fridge. A few minutes later I tried to extract it from the mould. It wouldn't budge. In the end I had to hack it out, the texture being that of plasticine. I was deeply frustrated, and there was no one to ask why this had happened. Of course, I now know that the chocolate needed to be tempered, and probably of a better quality to start off with, too.

LONDON LIFE

At sixteen I escaped the confines of the convent and moved to a London day school. But this liberation was tinged with huge sadness, for this was the year that my father died unexpectedly. He drowned while swimming alone in the rocky Atlantic waters in the Gambia, where he was working at the time. This was a shocking event for all the family, and brought us closer than ever. Overnight my mother had to become the main breadwinner. We all did what we could to help run the household and found many ways to celebrate life, most of them taking the form of cooking and eating delicious meals.

My parents were probably the first generation of 'foodies' as we know them today. They had grown up in the Second World War and endured rationing, and I can remember them describing the sense of joy and liberation at reading Elizabeth David's *A Book of Mediterranean Food*. Ingredients such as olive oil and Parmesan are deeply ingrained in our family's DNA, but they were new and exotic in post-war Britain. Throughout the 60s the whole family headed to Soho after attending Sunday mass at St Etheldreda's Church in the city, to buy packets of spaghetti wrapped in deep blue paper. We would be given small matchbox-sized Torrone nougat wrapped in rice paper by the kind family who ran Parmigiani's Italian deli. African and Middle Eastern dishes were regularly served up at the table and it was only when friends came for tea that we realised we were not conventional in our tastes. I also had a rather precocious enjoyment of wine, and was allowed my own thimble-sized wine glass. On special occasions, when a nice bottle was opened, I got to taste it. It gave me an early appreciation of wine and helped to develop my taste buds and olfactory sense.

My sisters and I studied at Mary Datchelor's School for Girls. There was a great young art teacher, Miss Newman, who encouraged us to try new things such as textile print- ing and photography, and typography classes on Saturdays at Camberwell School of Arts and Crafts. I loved those Saturdays, working with a letterpress typesetter who had decades of experience in his craft. I worked diligently on my portfolio and was offered a place on the foundation course at St Martin's School of Art. From St Martin's I embarked on a BA Fashion and Textile Degree course at Camberwell School of Arts and Crafts. I realised quickly that this was not my life's dream: the textile industry was in terminal decline, and it did not excite me that much.

The printmaking and photography departments beckoned. These were the days before computers and all our work was created using paper and pens. It was a great discipline, and though I am no technophobe it is still the way I work today. Years of art school were hugely important in developing my visual aesthetic. The design side of Rococo is second nature to me, and I am still the originator of almost every piece of artwork and the overall brand identity.

HARRODS

Given my family situation, I needed to earn money to exist as a student and eke out my meagre grant. I visited my old convent school friend Nicky Cousins, who was working in Harrods Chocolate Department while studying. As I waited for her to break for lunch I got lost in a reverie, breathing in the wonderful smells, looking at the displays and taking in the atmosphere. I was brought back to earth by the voice of the young and extremely handsome confectionery department buyer asking, 'Would you like a job?' A few weeks later I was in a white coat, working under the guiding hand of benign grandmother Edie, and together we manned the tuck shop where staff bought candy bars and mass-market pre-boxed chocolates. My first customer was tall, ruggedly handsome and beautifully dressed. 'I want the biggest box of Milk Tray you've got!' Why would he come to Harrods to buy this, when he could choose any of the beautifully packaged handmade chocolates on offer? However, it was not for me to question his judgment, so I smiled sweetly and packed the box in a bag. As he walked away Edie announced that he was Michael Caine, who came in every year to buy them for his mum's birthday. 'They're her favourites!', Edie told me. Sadly Sir Michael's mother died some years ago, but he has been and remains a regular Rococo customer.

I was transferred to work on another counter the following week, with one of Edie's fellow old-timers. I will call her 'H'. She was a bitter soul, who ruled her domain with a rod of iron and was the antithesis of everything one might want as a customer coming into the world's most famous department store. One transaction under her watch was particularly memorable – a Mars bar sold to a tourist who had the temerity to ask for a carrier bag. 'H' snatched the bag from my hand as I was about to hand it over, shrieking 'You can't give a carrier bag just for a Mars bar!' as if this were the deadliest sin in the book. Once the bemused customer had left, 'H' turned to me and explained, 'They only want the bag as a souvenir to prove that they've been to Harrods, and a Mars bar is the cheapest thing in the store!' So what, I thought. Why not let them advertise the fact that they had been in Harrods and bought something, however small? I eventually graduated to the fresh cream chocolate counter, the height of luxury in the early '80s. The chocolates were mainly Belgian, filled with rich, sweet whipped butter cream, and they were very perishable, so each box would be packed for the customer as they waited, causing long queues. This was seen as part of the experience, and the customers were terribly polite. When their turn came they would often ask for 'an assortment', a bit of everything. As a young upstart I had the temerity to suggest that since this was the typical buying pattern, perhaps we could have a fast-track line for ready-boxed assortments, to ease the queues. My boss would not hear of it. Trying to come up with a solution that would improve customer experience was the seed of an entrepreneurial idea. It is not always possible to dispense with queues, but it is important to acknowledge the fact that customers are patiently waiting, and give them a great experience when they get to the front of the line. I continued to work there for a couple of years, until one day I arrived with a radical haircut from the Vidal Sassoon Academy, the chicest place to go for all of us impoverished students. It was a short punky crop: the back was red, and the front was green. The boss did not look happy and I was told that if I came into work like that again, I would no longer have a job. The time had come to call it a day. My time at Harrods had been enlightening and I had learnt a lot about selling chocolate, but knew there was room for a radically different retail approach: an indulgent, fantastical one, a chocolate paradise. Why would anyone choose to be put through ritual humiliation when you want to be welcomed into a fantasy world of chocolate and have someone tend to your every whim? I started to dream about having my own shop.

AN EPIPHANY

After graduating, I set up an interior painting business with my art school friend Frank Taylor, but though the concept was fun the business struggled. I was listening to the radio one day when I heard an advertisement: the Manpower Services Commission was funding a course for people who wanted to start their own business. It was then that I had my light bulb moment. I wanted to start my own business and knew exactly what it would be: my dream chocolate shop. I was interviewed and offered a place on the ten-week course. It was a great introduction to business. During one of our role-play sessions, I was asked for the name of my business. The name *Rococo* was a wonderful accident. It just tripped off my tongue, and the dictionary definition sealed my fate:

Derived from the French word rocaille, meaning ornamentation, shell and scroll work, asymmetric. 18th century design style. Florid to the point of bad taste.

By the end of the course I had perfected my business plan and was ready to seek funding for my mad scheme. Purely out of courtesy, the first person I saw was my local bank manager, where I had held my student account. I was taken off guard when he said that he thought it an excellent plan. He would be happy to help and give me the loan. There was, of course, a sting in the tail. He needed security; what could I offer? I did not have a penny to my name. When I told my mother about the meeting, she said she would guarantee the loan by putting up the family home as collateral. My brother also offered to fund the down payment. This was an astonishing act of faith from both of them, risking all the family's assets on my venture. It certainly had the effect of motivating me to make the business succeed.

THE FIRST SHOP: A CHOCOLATE PARADISE

Armed with a little knowledge, and a dangerous passion for chocolate, I opened the first Rococo shop on the King's Road in Chelsea at Easter in 1983, at the age of 23. This was the moment I had been waiting for all my life and I was excited and nervous in equal measure. The decor in the first shop was wild and extremely camp. Working with Frank Taylor and Kitty Arden (who now designs Prestat's packaging), I created the theatrical backdrop for Rococo. We stippled the walls with scumble glaze and I commissioned a sugar chandelier. Frank painted a beautiful ornate ceiling, a homage to Botticelli's *Birth of Venus* with cherubs and clouds. From the minute the shop opened I was adopted by a charming couple, Leo and Philippa Bernard, who owned Chelsea Rare Books. Leo, my very first customer, was standing outside with their spaniel Tess on the morning I opened, just before Easter. The shop was filled with handmade eggs from a chocolate factory that supplied Charbonnel et Walker, and they rapidly sold out, but the wonderful Raymond Matthias – who had a garage filled with Belgian bunnies and Easter treats – dropped in daily to replenish supplies. We were all very happy.

Selling bags of chocolate in Bonnington Square.
Production still from 'Radio Dog' by Nick Turvey.
Photograph by Mark Prizeman.

People started to ask what the shop would be after Easter; pop-up shops didn't exist then, and it was not seen as a viable business model to have a chocolate shop for 52 weeks of the year. The summer that followed was long and hot. The landlords put up scaffolding outside the building, so we were invisible and had the most dreadful time financially. We had started out in the middle of a long recession; Margaret Thatcher had her teeth bared and inflation roared away. Pretty soon I had to pay over 25% interest on my loan. I felt like I was running just to keep still. The only thing to do was have fun, so when the shop was quiet, friends popped in with Pimms and we would have a party, or cook lunches and hold board meetings where we voted on things like 'Shall we get a shop cat?'. The answer was 'yes', and we found a beautiful stray at Battersea Dog's Home, named her Coco, and put her to work as pest control officer. She was a beautiful, dignified and affectionate cat with many good friends, including Ali MacGraw, who thought she was a 'just adorable kitty'. Sadly, someone reported her to the council, who issued her marching orders on the grounds of health and safety. Coco spent the rest of her life in the suburbs of South London, dining on fillet steak.

A jumble sale in Bonnington Square gardens, circa 1982, since transformed into the beautiful Bonnington Square Pleasure Garden.

BONNINGTON SQUARE

When I was finishing art school, just before I opened the first shop, my best friend Frank Taylor told me he and some friends were squatting in a house in Vauxhall's Bonnington Square. It was a small square of empty Victorian properties that were more or less derelict. The minute I visited, I fell in love with the square. It was like something out of a Hitchcock movie or Ealing comedy – very run down, with no trees or plants, yet buzzing with musicians, writers, anarchists, hippies and painters. At Frank's suggestion I moved in, without a moment's hesitation. The house was extremely basic: one bathroom had the only hot water tank and we'd carry buckets of hot water down to the kitchen to wash up. I dressed the part of the respectable young lady and left the house early in the morning to meet suppliers, in an effort to show that I was trustworthy and, more to the point, creditworthy, then headed to the shop. It was a Jekyll and Hyde existence. My shop neighbours thought I was very posh – some boys

from a nearby shoe shop, Robot, convinced themselves that I was the daughter of a lord, and others swallowed my story that I had had an affair with one of Thatcher's naughty-boy ministers and the shop was my pay-off – they fell for it hook, line and sinker. It was a time of huge change; the era of punk, when computers were just becoming affordable to the masses, and life was notching up several gears. I met many brilliant and talented people, many of whom have remained good friends: Scott Crolla and Georgina Godley, who had a chic and anarchic clothes shop called Crolla in Dover St; Sebastian Conran and his siblings Jasper, Tom, Sophie and Ned; a slighter older, more sophisticated crowd included Doug Hamilton (vision-ary creative director behind Orange Hutchinson, among others) and Brian Boylan (now Chairman of Wolff Olins) and the bohemian Chelsea arty set of Paul Kasmin, Danny Moynihan and Bill Amberg. All these people seamlessly merged into the London scene in which I belonged.

Sunday Times *Colour Supplement circa 1984. Lying on a freezing cold basement floor in midwinter!*

A 'SALON DE THÉ' SUMMER

I attended many art openings, tamer affairs than the club and gig nights I'd been used to during art school, with plenty of free-flowing, cheap Bulgarian wine. One such opening was a show of furniture and sculpture by Tom Dixon, Mark Brazier Jones and Nick Jones, who went on to form Creative Salvage. The pieces were bits of scrap metal welded together; junk recycled into objects. Their slogan was 'never leave a skip unturned'. In spite of being made from ephemeral materials with little craftsmanship, they were compelling as works of art and had a raw energy and anarchic quality. I bought a piece I particularly liked for £25, titled 'The African Queen's Throne'. Tom dropped it off at Rococo the next day, and was amused at the juxtaposition of the rough metal object with the pristine white marble floor of the shop and the pink cherub interior. One day I suggested Tom make me a fancy swivelling office chair. On delivery, Tom joked that I was the first person to have bought two things from him, which made me his first Patron. We had the idea of turning Rococo into a Salon de Thé and gallery space for the summer.

I knew we would not be busy selling chocolate – the season was September to Easter – so I was happy to find another use for the space. The Salon de Thé creative team comprised André Dubreuil with his statuesque assistant Joy Ayode, who were interior designers and specialist paint finishers, Georgina of Crolla, who designed the costumes for the waitresses (I was to be the Madame), and Tom Dixon and Mark Brazier Jones, who made the furniture. The identity of the shop was transformed; gone were Frank's cherubs, and the sugar chandelier, now grey and dusty, came down. I was sad, but there was no looking back. The shop was populated with sculptural furniture that was neither safe nor comfortable to sit on, yet we served an Afternoon Tea of fine leaf teas, ice creams, and homemade scones and sandwiches. The Salon was a huge success, with global press coverage and articles about us in glossy magazines, including Italian *Vogue* and *The Face*.

A NEW ERA

It was time to lose the dated pink and gold cherub wrapping paper. André lent
me his old French books on design, beautiful leather-bound editions made from
a series of copper plate engravings from A Morel et Cie, which was the birth of
the Rococo monochrome period. I designed a black and white pattern using one
of the pages, turning it into a repeating motif with the bird of paradise. At a party
held by Leo and Philippa I met Robin de Beaumont, their elegant and recherché
antiquarian bookseller colleague. He had a very good eye, not only for beautiful girls,
but also for fine volumes. He came to the shop one day clasping a small red book, a
chocolate mould trade catalogue from the late 1890s. In it were beautifully engraved
line drawings of fantasy creatures, Easter eggs, chocolate bars and all the things
that were on sale at that time to French confectioners and chocolatiers. The images
were equally compelling: scallop shells, lobsters, oysters and fish, all deeply Rococo
motifs, as well as heads and animals. It was not cheap, indeed it was priced at most
of a month's wages for me at the time, but I was seduced. Robin kindly gave me a
discount and I remember his parting words: 'You will not regret this. I know you
will do something extraordinary with it'. I had the idea of making a sheet of tissue
paper using my favourite images from the book. Fortunately all the images were out
of copyright, as they were over 50 years old. I photocopied the images I liked most
and glued them on to a sheet of paper. The whole process took about 10 minutes.
Gordon, the printer, took one look at it and said, 'I think it's just brilliant, it's going
to look very beautiful!' He took away the rough layout and had a copper roller made
with the designs etched into it and the enduring Rococo brand was born; the blue
and white patterns that everyone now associates with us.

Despite all I have said about friends and parties, I worked very hard, getting up early,
diligently keeping the books and working most days behind the counter. At Easter
there were queues out on to the street, and on our busiest days we would serve a
thousand customers. At the end of those long days, we would crawl down to the
basement and collapse in a heap, revive ourselves with a glass of Champagne, then
set about filling the empty shelves for the next day. My mother and her friends
would offer support, help pack eggs and feed us hot cross buns on Good Friday.
On Easter Sunday, we would have a celebratory brunch behind locked doors for
everyone who had helped the season go off with a bang, followed by three days
of complete rest, while the shop was closed. That was the time when Rococo
had the monopoly on designer chocolates. In the 1980s and early 1990s there
was no one making chocolate on a small scale in London, just the institutions like
Charbonnel et Walker, Prestat and the big department stores. We were offering
something unique – wit and beauty in chocolate – but it took ten years to break
even. The day I persuaded the bank to hand the deeds back to my mother was one
of the best days of my life, and a huge weight lifted from my shoulders.

*Black and white design,
using a Rococo bird
motif from the antique*
Ornaments Tirés,
*published by A Morel &
Cie Editeurs.*

THE CHOCOLATE SOCIETY

In the 1980s a supplier, Robin Dalgliesh, introduced me to an exciting new product he was importing, a small black tin box of wrapped chocolate from Valrhona, designed by Sonia Rykiel. The first French designer chocolate had arrived. Valrhona produced well-crafted, exceptional dark chocolate, cleverly borrowing wine terminology from their wine-making neighbours in the Rhone Valley to market their products. In 1987 Robin sadly died of a rare blood disorder. Alan Porter, a fellow chocolate distributor of Robin's, took over importing Valrhona, and we became colleagues and friends. There was a convivial dinner that culminated in a tasting of fine single malts, which were offered with the chocolate. They came from The Malt Whisky Society, and were a perfect foil for the Valrhona chocolate. I realised that what we lacked in the UK was a chocolate society. Alan and I decided to establish one. I designed the cocoa pod logo and, with our friend David Pearl, we wrote the copy expounding the joys of real chocolate. The Chocolate Society was launched in 1991 as a members organisation, introducing the delights of great chocolate to enthusiasts with talks, tastings, demonstrations and hands-on chocolate making, and access to chocolate by post.

I visited the Valrhona Ecole de Grand Chocolat and had my grounding in the theory and practice of artisan chocolate production. Alan and his wife Nicola converted one of their outbuildings into a chocolate kitchen and started to make ganaches, which were sold through the Society, then in their own shop. I realised that I had taken my eye of the ball for too long. I needed to put my energy back into Rococo and rise to the emerging competition, so I started producing small quantities of house truffles using Valrhona Manjari, cream and butter.

MEETING JAMES

One summer's day in 1992 I was helping Ted McNamara – neighbour, wise man and Alexander Technique teacher – prepare food for a garden party he was hosting. It was the last thing I felt like doing, as I was exhausted from a long day's work lifting tons of chocolate, but I had committed to it and was not going to let him down. After several hours of chopping and cooking I returned home for a soak in the bath, and dressed up to go and put in an appearance. The party had started and there were tables of food and drink and people milling around. I was introduced to James Booth, a tall slim conventional-looking young man, who looked a little lost. He had just qualified in Acupuncture at the School of Chinese Medicine, and I offered to give him a guided tour through the labyrinthine garden, in its full mid-summer glory. I was so tired but James, for all that he was not my type (and I was engaged to someone else), was entertaining company. We talked about wild mushrooms, particularly morels. James knew they were called *morilles* in French and did not believe me when I said I thought they were simply *morel* in English. As I left the party James asked for my address, telling me that he was going to China for his postgraduate studies and would send me a postcard. I was surprised to receive a letter the next week: he had looked up the translation and said I was correct in my assertion of *morel*, and, would I like to go on a date before he left for China. He had not given a phone number, so I was compelled to write back. This led to a whirlwind romance, and we met up in Bali that November to marry in Ubud. The marriage was in the traditional Balinese Hindu Animist tradition, where the bridegroom 'kidnaps' the bride, they go to the volcano, and return to be blessed by the priest. Our guests at the blessing were our host family, a gamalan band and our Australian friend Derek. We later officially tied the knot at Brixton registry office with our families, and held a summer party a year after we had met, in the same garden, with all our friends.

ROCOCO FLAVOURS

I have drawn and painted for as long as I can remember, having been encouraged by my parents to develop a good eye and a curious mind, and this creativity enables me to visualise colours and flavours. I always assumed that everyone could do this, but I am finally coming to understand that it is a gift. I use it when dreaming up new flavours for Rococo bars, such as our Violet bars and wafers: I looked for years to find a pure violet oil that was deep and fruity, not sweet and soapy like Parma Violets, that could be blended with our dark chocolate, eventually collaborating with a perfume house who made the perfect violet distillation.

My childhood memories inspired our Basil and Persian Lime bars and wafers. I have a lasting memory of raiding the kitchen cupboard, not for sweet things but for the dried black Persian limes. I would crack them open and pick out the tar-like treacly black fruit; intensely sour and deeply satisfying.

We were the first London chocolatiers to make sea salt, chilli, rosemary and black pepper chocolates in the early 90s. The idea for sea salt milk chocolate, imitated by chocolate makers worldwide, came to me when crystals of sea salt settled on my lips as I was walking along the beach in Cornwall, licking clotted cream ice cream. It subtly enhanced the sweetness – test this yourself by adding a flake of sea salt to your next taste of milk chocolate, or a piece of melon.

When we create our recipes, the act of balancing the chocolate with the flavouring is a fine one. We want the chocolate notes to sing out with the flavours, creating a harmonious entity that is greater than the sum of its parts, with no dominant note. To help us achieve this, we combined our house blend of Grenada organic chocolate with other couvertures, as pure Grenada is otherwise too dominant when blended with other flavours.

THE ART OF CHOCOLATE MAKING

To start production of our own handmade house truffles back in 1991, we converted a room on the ground floor of our Bonnington Square house into a kitchen to be used only for making chocolate; just a large marble table for tempering and a bain-marie for melting. It was a spiritual homecoming, crafting Rococo chocolates within a stone's throw of Vauxhall Gardens, the home of Rococo London in the eighteenth century. We experimented, tried out new flavours, and made beautiful one-off hand-painted figurines, eggs, rabbits, fish and hearts and our Artisan bars and house truffles. I hired our first part-time chocolatier, Jo Gaskell, a psychotherapist from a culinary family (her sister is cookery writer Jocelyn Dimbleby). Although she had not worked with chocolate before, she was a complete natural. Soon she was technically better than me. Our second chocolatier was Ruth Morgan, an artistic neighbour who took to the painting like the proverbial duck to water. One day a young pastry chef called Gerard Coleman came to see me in the shop, after reading my book *The Chocolate Companion* (a directory of chocolate makers around the world) and asked me if I would be his mentor. I suggested he learn with one of the masters in Europe. After a year in Brussels with Pierre Marcolini, Gerard returned and asked if he could join Rococo as our first full-time chocolatier. We were still working from our tiny kitchen, so it was a leap of faith, but it was great to have someone with the skills of a true pastry chef. Output grew and we developed a range of flavoured ganache prototypes, which we invited Nigel Slater to taste – he was highly enthusiastic.

I had a baby, was pregnant with my second child, and was juggling life as wife, mother and businesswoman. Now I had a headstrong young man on board who wanted daily meetings, and presented me with a vast shopping list of expensive equipment. Eventually I had to let him go and follow his dreams. I wished him well as he set up L'Artisan du Chocolat round the corner from the King's Road.

Now I had serious competition. The same book brought me Richard Von Geusau, a South African accountant who wanted to be a chocolatier. We met a few times and he set up his own boutique chocolaterie near Cape Town. We're still in touch and he has a very successful business, Von Geusau Chocolates. Subsequently, a pastry chef working with Marco Pierre White came to me and proposed that we commission him to make a couple of limited edition chocolates for Chocolate Week. They were a great success, so, with the chocolate bit between his teeth, Paul A Young went to open a shop in Camden Passage. A plethora of bright young talent has emerged on to the chocolate scene in the last decade and it's a great thing: London is one of the most creative and original cities for chocolate-making in the world, and I am proud to have been a part of preparing the ground for this flowering. It has also spurred me on to enhance what I do.

In 2004 we opened our second shop in Marylebone High St and it was an instant success. Suddenly turnover doubled and we relocated the chocolate kitchen and mail order service to a large industrial loft in South London. The third shop and chocolate school in Motcomb St followed in late 2007. Together with our chocolatier, I run chocolate classes at weekends and we make fresh batches of ganache during the week, which form the Rococo Couture collection and change with every season. They keep for around two weeks, as there are no preservatives added, only butter, cream and pure ingredients such as lemon, passion fruit, mango, rose, lychee, salted caramel, violet, raspberry, cherry, saffron and cardamom, Grenada Rum, or Islay single malt. Laurent Couchaux, our chocolatier until 2011, came up with a wonderful range of ganaches. He submitted two for the Academy of Chocolate awards and received gold medals for both, and more recently won another couple of golds for ganaches made with our Grenada Chocolate Company couverture. Laurent returned to France, to spend more time with his children after ten years of being an ex-pat, and in early 2012 Barry Johnson joined us from the Michelin-starred Coworth Park as our new Prof du Choc.

ETHICAL COCOA

The future of cocoa concerns me greatly. Most cocoa farmers are over 70, and the young are moving to the cities. Unless we pay the real price for cocoa, we may have no chocolate in 10 years' time. I want to be a part of reversing that trend in our own small way, and one of the most exciting projects we have embarked on is a joint venture with the Grenada Chocolate Company. The first time I came across their organic chocolate was when it appeared on my desk, having been deposited by the fleet-footed Mr Clayton, neighbour of the GCC and frequent visitor to the UK. It was clear that it had some pedigree. Not only was it made from the world famous Trinitario beans, it was made in situ using antique machines and solar power and, crucially, it was reversing the terms of trade, with all the value being added at the start of the production chain. The cocoa is ground into chocolate up the road from where it grows, and much of the chocolate makes its way into our Artisan bars. Our most recent project is the creation of Gru Grococo, made with a single day's harvest from our land. They were fermented, dried, roasted and ground in one small batch, to our own special recipe with no added vanilla. A limited edition was shipped on a square-rigged brigantine from Grenada to London in spring 2012 using nothing but wind power. It is the fruition of a dream and I believe the way forward in the world of cocoa and chocolate, and social entrepreneurship.

I think it is true to say that most of us love chocolate, but it is one of the most temperamental ingredients to work with. I want to share with you the dark secrets of what makes chocolate behave – or misbehave – the way it does, and demystify its nature. There is so much joy in sharing chocolate with your loved ones, and it is even more intensely felt if you have made them yourself, so delve into the recipes for our award-winning chocolates and confectionery, and our favourite pastries and cakes. You'll discover the key principles of chocolate-making in indulgent and beautiful detail, from tempering and decorating to making the perfect truffle: the secrets of Rococo, told for the very first time.

BON—
BONS,
BITES &
BARS

CLASSIC TRUFFLES

Making your own truffles is very simple. The secret is to enjoy them while they are fresh, so they are perfect for making at home.

Makes 80 truffles

Special equipment
15cm square baking tin or rigid plastic box lined with clingfilm
Disposable piping bag

Ingredients
210g Grenada Chocolate Co. chocolate (71% cocoa solids), broken into pieces
200ml whipping cream
50g liquid glucose or honey
50g softened unsalted butter, diced
Flavourless oil, for greasing
500g good quality dark or milk chocolate, tempered (see p226–228), for dipping
Cocoa powder, chopped toasted nuts or vermicelli, to decorate (optional)

Melt the chocolate in a bowl over a bain-marie and set it aside.

Place the cream and glucose or honey in a small heavy-based saucepan and gently heat until it is almost boiling. Remove from the heat and leave for 2 minutes to cool slightly. Stir a third of the hot cream into the melted chocolate with a rubber spatula. As the mixture starts to thicken, stir the next third into the mixture, and by the addition of final third you will have a beautifully smooth and glossy emulsion. Beat the butter into the emulsion, or blend it in with a stick blender, until it has been fully incorporated.

Pour the ganache mixture into a shallow container, spread it out evenly and place a sheet of clingfilm over the surface. Leave it at room temperature for 30 minutes–1 hour to firm up. Spoon it into a piping bag and pipe chocolate kisses (see page 326–327) on to greaseproof paper. Secure the corners of the paper with a little bit of ganache, so the paper doesn't move, then put the truffles back into the fridge to firm up again. Dip the chilled truffle kisses one by one into the tempered chocolate, using a dipping fork or your hands, making sure they are evenly coated, then roll them in cocoa powder, chopped toasted nuts or vermicelli. Place them on a baking tray lined with a silicone mat or greaseproof paper and leave to set.

Store in an airtight container – they will keep for a week – or place them in cellophane bags to make beautiful gifts.

CHOCOLATE SLABS

You can be as simple or elaborate as you like with these slabs. Plunder your store cupboard for herbs and spices, dried fruits and peels, or shop around for fresh nuts or more exotic ingredients. I am lucky enough to live close to Persepolis in Peckham, where you can find tangy red dried barberries, dried limes and rose petals, all of which lend themselves perfectly to these slabs.

Special equipment

33 x 23cm Swiss roll tin

Ingredients

For dark chocolate slabs

500g good quality dark chocolate

Flavourless oil, for greasing

5g chilli flakes

10g dried barberries (see p249 for stockists)

1g dried rose petals (see p88)

For salted milk chocolate slabs

500g good quality milk chocolate

Flavourless oil, for greasing

2–3g sea salt

For fruity milk chocolate slabs

500g good quality milk chocolate

Flavourless oil, for greasing

8g freeze-dried passion fruit pieces
(see p249 for stockists)

20g Rococo or Home Chocolate Factory
chocolate-coated popping candy

6g freeze-dried yogurt pieces
(see p249 for stockists)

For white chocolate slabs

500g good quality white chocolate

Flavourless oil, for greasing

20g freeze-dried raspberry pieces
(see p249 for stockists)

2g sugared mint pieces (see p249 for stockists)

The method is the same for all slabs: temper the chocolate, using the tablier method (see page 227) or seeding method (page 228). Lightly grease the Swiss roll tin with a little oil and line it with clingfilm – the oil will help the clingfilm stick to the tray as the chocolate sets, but make sure the oil doesn't come into contact with the chocolate.

Pour the tempered chocolate into the tray and spread it out with a palette knife. Tap the tray on the work surface a couple of times, keeping it level, to even out the surface of the chocolate and get rid of any air bubbles. Immediately sprinkle the chocolate with the toppings suggested to the left, or your own choice of toppings: the possibilities are endless.

Leave the chocolate to set in a cool, dry place for 2 hours, to allow the chocolate to crystallise, which will give it its distinctive crisp snap. Carefully lift the chocolate slab and clingfilm out of the tray. Remove the clingfilm from the slabs before gently breaking them into large shards. Store in an airtight container – they will keep well for a week or two – or place them in cellophane bags to make beautiful gifts.

SALTED LEMON CARAMEL BATONS

This is a variation on the salted caramel theme, which we use in the Billionaire's Shortbread (see page 184). It is a classic caramel; melting and buttery with the delicate flavours of lemon and salt coming through on the palate. After making and dipping, this bundle of sticks reminded us of faggots from childhood fairy tales like Hansel and Gretel.

Makes 36 sticks

Special equipment

18 x 18cm stainless steel frame

Probe thermometer

Ingredients

200ml whipping cream

A large pinch of sea salt

3 unwaxed lemons

15g liquid glucose

175g caster sugar

50g softened unsalted butter, diced

500g Grenada Chocolate Co. chocolate (71% cocoa solids), tempered (see p226), for dipping

Lemon or Orange Powder (see p94), to decorate

Place the cream and salt in a small heavy-based saucepan and gently heat until it is almost boiling. Remove from the heat and grate the zest from the lemons directly into the cream. Cover with clingfilm or a close-fitting lid and leave to infuse for 30 minutes.

Place the glucose in a clean and grease-free heavy-based saucepan over a medium heat. Once hot, put a third of the sugar in the pan. Heat the sugar, shaking the pan regularly, and stir until the sugar melts. Add another third of the sugar to the pan and let it melt, stirring with a wooden spoon, then finally add the remaining third. Once all the sugar is in the pan and caramelising, the temperature will rise quite quickly and the sugar will darken to a golden caramel colour.

Take the pan off the heat when the sugar reaches this stage and add the butter, piece by piece, stirring well after each addition. Strain the infused cream through a sieve, pressing out all the cream from the zest with the back of a wooden spoon. Discard the zest, and pour the infused cream on to the caramel. Put the pan back over a medium heat and bring to the boil, stirring constantly, until the mixture reaches 118°C. Pour the caramel mixture into the frame set on top of a silicone mat or greaseproof paper and spread it out evenly. Store it in a cool, dry place (maximum 18°C) or at room temperature, to firm up.

Remove the frame and, using a stepped palette knife, spread a 1mm layer of tempered chocolate over the caramel. Once it has set, turn the slab of caramel over and cut the caramel into 9cm long and 1cm wide fingers. Dip them into the tempered chocolate one by one using two dipping forks. Place them on a baking tray lined with a silicone mat or greaseproof paper, sprinkle with Lemon or Orange Powder and leave to set. The faggots will keep well for up to 2 weeks if covered in tempered chocolate and kept in a cool, dry place.

COFFEE & LEMON TRUFFLES

These truffles have a wonderful flavour; a soft caramel texture and a lemony tang, with a gentle hint of coffee. They remind me of Dutch Hopjes sweets, or espressos with lemon zest, which are served in bars in Rome or Sicily. They need to be made two days before eating.

Makes 80 truffles

Special equipment

18 x 18cm stainless steel frame

Ingredients

500g good quality dark or milk chocolate, tempered (see p226–228), for chablon and dipping

135ml freshly squeezed lemon juice (you will need approximately 3 lemons)

22g freshly crushed (not ground) medium-roast Arabica coffee beans

A pinch of Fleur de Sel salt (we use Halen Môn from Anglesey)

52g liquid glucose or honey

390g Valrhona Caramelia chocolate (see p249 for stockists)

75g softened unsalted butter, diced

Crushed coffee beans, edible gold powder and Rococo argent assortment dragées, to decorate (optional see p249)

Make a chablon base (see page 229) with the tempered chocolate, and place the frame on top of the chablon before it sets.

Place the lemon juice and crushed coffee beans in a small heavy-based saucepan and gently heat until it is almost boiling. Remove the pan from the heat, cover with clingfilm or a close-fitting lid and leave to infuse for 30 minutes. Pour the coffee and lemon juice through a sieve into a clean saucepan and add the salt and glucose or honey. Warm gently over a low heat to dissolve the salt, then remove from the heat.

Melt the Caramelia chocolate in a bowl over a bain-marie. Remove the bowl from the bain-marie and stir about a third of the hot liquid into the melted chocolate with a rubber spatula. As the mixture starts to thicken, stir the next third into the mixture, and by the addition of the final third you will have a smooth and glossy ganache. Beat the butter into the emulsion, or blend it in with a stick blender, until it has been fully incorporated.

Pour the ganache mixture into the frame set on top of the chablon, spread it out evenly and store it in a cool, dry place (maximum 18°C) or at room temperature, ideally overnight, to firm up to a butter-like consistency.

Remove the frame and cut the ganache into roughly 2cm cubes. Dip the cubes one by one in the tempered chocolate, using a dipping fork. The chablon acts as a foundation, so the ganache is not too soft to dip. Put them on a baking tray lined with a silicone mat or greaseproof paper to set. Decorate the dipped chocolates before they set with crushed coffee beans, dusted with gold powder. When they are set, you could sprinkle with silver dragées.

The truffles will keep well for up to a week if covered in tempered chocolate and kept in a cool, dry place.

MILK CHOCOLATE CINNAMON TRUFFLES

These are silky smooth, with a delicate flavour of cinnamon and vanilla – a lovely way of getting children to taste a flavour other than straight milk chocolate. You could also use other spices in it if you wish: nutmeg, cardamom, star anise, liquorice root or bark.

Makes 30–40 truffles

Special equipment

15cm square baking tin or rigid plastic box lined with clingfilm
Probe thermometer
Disposable piping bag fitted with 5mm round nozzle

Ingredients

250g good quality milk chocolate (40% cocoa solids), broken into pieces
130ml whipping cream
15g liquid glucose or honey
30g caster sugar
1 cinnamon stick, crushed
½ vanilla pod, split lengthways
40g softened unsalted butter, diced
300g good quality milk chocolate, tempered (see p226–228), for dipping
Icing sugar (flavoured with ground cinnamon if you wish), cocoa powder, or chopped nuts, to decorate

Melt the chocolate in a bowl over a bain-marie. Set aside.

Place the cream and glucose or honey in a small heavy-based saucepan and gently heat until it is almost boiling. Remove from the heat and set aside. Place a clean and grease-free heavy-based saucepan over a medium heat. Once hot, put all of the sugar in the pan with the crushed cinnamon stick and split vanilla pod. Heat the sugar, shaking the pan regularly, and stir until the sugar melts.

Remove the pan from the heat when the caramel has darkened to a golden colour and pour the warm cream into the caramel, stirring with a rubber spatula to combine. Be careful, as it will bubble and spit. Pass the mixture through a sieve into a clean heatproof bowl and let it cool to 60°C. Stir a third of the caramel cream into the melted chocolate with a rubber spatula. As the mixture thickens, stir the next third in, and by the addition of the final third you will have a smooth and glossy ganache. Beat in the butter, until it has been fully incorporated. Pour the ganache mixture into a shallow container, spread it out evenly and place a sheet of clingfilm over the surface. Leave it at room temperature for 30 minutes–1 hour to firm up.

Spoon it into a piping bag and pipe into long logs on a baking tray covered with non-stick baking paper (use a little ganache to stick the corners of the paper to the tray, to prevent it moving while you are piping).

Leave to set overnight in a cool place. Cut to size when set, then dip them one by one into the tempered chocolate, using two dipping forks. Make sure they are evenly coated, then roll them in icing sugar, cocoa powder or chopped nuts. Place them on a baking tray lined with a silicone mat or greaseproof paper and leave to set. The truffles will keep well for up to a week if covered in tempered chocolate and kept in a cool dry place.

CHAMPAGNE TRUFFLES

Universally popular, these are romantic and luxurious, and surprisingly easy to make. Personally I would not waste my Krug on this, but that is up to you, of course! Most chocolatiers use Marc de Champagne, as it has a more intense flavour.

Makes 40 truffles

Special equipment
18 x 18cm stainless steel frame,
15cm square baking tin or rigid
plastic box lined with clingfilm

Ingredients
200g good quality dark chocolate
(or 100g dark and 100g milk),
broken into pieces
90ml Champagne or Prosecco
1 tbsp brandy or vodka (I use
homemade damson vodka)
1 tsp honey
100ml crème fraîche
500g good quality milk or dark
chocolate, tempered
(see p226–228), for dipping
Freeze-dried raspberries blitzed
and then mixed with icing sugar
1kg icing sugar, for dusting
Flavourless oil, for greasing

Melt the chocolate for the truffles in a bowl over a bain-marie. Set aside.

Place the champagne and brandy or vodka in a small heavy-based saucepan, add the honey, and gently heat until it is almost boiling. Stir about a third of the booze into the melted chocolate with a rubber spatula. As the mixture starts to thicken, stir the next third into the mixture and by the addition of the final third you will have a smooth and glossy ganache. Beat the crème fraîche into the emulsion, or blend it in with a stick blender, until it has been fully incorporated.

Place the frame on the oiled tray and line it with clingfilm. Pour the ganache mixture and spread it out evenly with a palette knife and store it in a cool, dry place (maximum 18°C) or at room temperature, ideally overnight, to firm up to a butter-like consistency.

Release the ganache from the frame or container by taking a hot knife around the edge, removing the clingfilm, and place it on a clean work surface. Cut it into 40 equal-sized cubes, and dip in the sugar and eat immediately.

If you want to give the truffles as a gift, they will need to be dipped in the tempered chocolate before the icing sugar. To do this, place the icing sugar in a shallow baking tin. Dip the chilled truffle cubes one by one into the tempered chocolate, using two dipping forks, and make sure they are evenly coated. Shake off any excess chocolate and drop the truffles into the icing sugar. Roll them until they are completely covered, and leave them in the tray for 5–10 minutes until the chocolate has started to harden. Place the truffles in a sieve and gently shake off the excess icing sugar.

Keep the truffles in a cool, dry place and eat within a day or two of making.

OLIVE OIL, LEMON & BASIL TRUFFLES

*This is one of our summer collection truffles created by chocolatier Laurent Couchaux,
a heavenly marriage of peppery olive oil and fresh citrus notes from lemon and basil, with
white chocolate. It makes an excellent 'extreme canapé' with Parmesan or Grana Padano
(see page 194). The ganache needs to be made a couple of days before eating.*

Makes 54 truffles

Special equipment
Probe thermometer
18 x 18cm stainless steel frame
Cocoa butter transfer sheets (see
p249 for stockists)

Ingredients
100ml whipping cream, plus extra
for topping up if needed
Peeled strips of zest and 30ml
juice from 1 lemon
500g dark couverture chocolate,
tempered (see p226–229), for
chablon and dipping
250g good quality white chocolate
A pinch of sea salt
20ml good quality, peppery extra
virgin olive oil
1 tsp basil oil

Place the cream in a heavy-based saucepan and heat it gently until it reaches boiling point. Put the lemon zest in a heatproof glass bowl and pour the hot cream over the zest. Leave it to cool to room temperature, cover and transfer the bowl to the fridge overnight to infuse. The next day, make a chablon base with the tempered chocolate (see page 229), and place the frame on top of the chablon before it sets.

Melt the white chocolate in a bowl over a bain-marie. Gently heat the infused cream with the salt in a saucepan or microwave until it reaches 70°C and strain it through a sieve, discarding the zest. You need 85ml of liquid; top up the infused cream with more cream if necessary. Remove the chocolate from the bain-marie and stir a third of the hot liquid into the melted chocolate with a rubber spatula. As the mixture starts to thicken, stir in the next third, and by the addition of the final third you will have a smooth and glossy ganache. Gradually stir in the warm lemon juice with a rubber spatula, followed by the olive and basil oils. Blend with a stick blender until the oil has been fully incorporated. Pour the ganache mixture into the frame set on top of the chablon, spread it out evenly and store it in a cool, dry place or at room temperature (maximum 18°C) overnight, to firm up to a butter-like consistency.

Remove the frame and cut the ganache into 3cm x 2cm rectangles. Dip them one by one into the tempered chocolate using a dipping fork. Put them on a baking tray lined with silicone paper. If you are using a cocoa-butter transfer sheet, place the sheet on to the dipped chocolates (see page 82) or just mark them with a fork and leave them to set for two hours before removing the transfer sheet to reveal the pattern.

The truffles will keep well for up to a week if covered in tempered chocolate and kept in a cool, dry place.

GOAT'S CHEESE GANACHE

My twelve expert tasters all loved this, even when they heard what the mystery ingredient was. It is light in texture and has an extremely subtle flavour, so subtle in fact that only one of the dozen tasters guessed it contained goat's cheese. Try serving it as an 'extreme canapé' (see page 194), quenelled on to sea salt chocolate wafers rather than rolled into truffle balls, or replacing the goat's cheese with camembert, taleggio or stilton, removing the rind and cutting it into pieces before adding to the cream.

Makes 30–40 truffles

Special equipment
18 x 18cm stainless steel frame, 15cm square baking tin or rigid plastic box lined with clingfilm

Ingredients
100g good quality dark chocolate (65–70% cocoa solids)
150ml whipping cream
50g fresh white rindless goat's cheese, cut into small pieces
Freshly ground black pepper, to taste
Finely ground sea salt, to taste
Unsweetened cocoa powder (optional)
Flavourless oil, for greasing

Melt the chocolate in a bowl over a bain-marie and set it aside. Place the cream in a small saucepan and heat gently until it is almost boiling, leave it to rest for 1 minute, then stir in the goat's cheese, black pepper and salt. Blend with a stick blender or beat to amalgamate the cheese with the cream, then stir a third of the cream mixture into the melted chocolate with a rubber spatula. As the mixture starts to thicken, stir in the next third, and by the final third you will have a beautifully smooth and glossy emulsion.

Pour the ganache mixture into the frame (oiled and sat on a baking tray) or container lined with clingfilm, spread it out evenly and store it in a cool, dry place (maximum 18°C) or at room temperature, ideally overnight, to firm up to a butter-like consistency.

To serve as a canapé, remove the ganache from the frame or container, and spread the chilled ganache on to sea salt chocolate wafers. Alternatively, remove the clingfilm (if used) and place the ganache on a clean work surface. Cut it into roughly 2cm cubes. Roll the cubes into balls with your hands (use latex gloves if you have them – it makes the job easier), or shape them into quenelles with two teaspoons, and dip each truffle into cocoa powder if you want. Set aside to set.

The truffles will keep well for 4–5 days covered and kept in the fridge.

FLORAL CREAM FONDANTS

Rose and violet creams, quintessential English delicacies, have that Marmite effect on people, inspiring passion and revulsion in equal measure. We love them and ensure we never run out of stock, as the consequences are simply unthinkable.

Makes 40–45 cream fondants

Ingredients

30ml double cream

1 tsp rose water, violet essence, other floral essence or syrup, or 1 drop of food-safe essential oil (to taste)

3 drops of red/lilac food colouring (optional)

1 medium egg white

½ tsp lemon juice

Approximately 420g icing sugar, sifted

300g Grenada Chocolate Co. chocolate (71% cocoa solids), tempered (see p226–228), for dipping

Crystallised Rose Petals (see p88) or Rainbow Sugar (see p92), to decorate

Place the double cream in a jug and add the rose water (or flavouring of choice) and food colouring, if using. The total quantity of liquid – the cream, flavouring and colouring – must not exceed 30ml. Place the jug on digital scales and start with 25ml of cream and add the flavour and colour before topping up to 30ml with the cream.

Beat the egg white with an electric hand whisk until it forms stiff peaks, then add the lemon juice, followed by 300g of the icing sugar and the flavoured and coloured (optional) cream, and beat until the mixture forms a stiff paste. If it is too loose, turn it out on to a very clean work surface and knead in the remaining icing sugar until the paste is smooth and stiff. Divide the paste into 15mm pieces, roll each one into a ball, then lightly flatten into 20mm-thick discs. Place on a tray lined with non-stick baking paper and leave to dry overnight.

Dip the discs one by one in the tempered chocolate, using a dipping fork. Place them on a baking tray covered with a silicone mat or greaseproof paper and decorate with Crystallised Rose Petals or Rainbow Sugar before they set. If you want to be professional about it, you can dip them in the chocolate twice: first just the base by hand which acts like a chablon, and then when the base is set, you dip the whole chocolate using the dipping fork, before decorating. Chill for an hour or two until set.

The floral cream fondants will keep well for up to 2 weeks if covered in tempered chocolate and kept in a cool, dry place.

SALTED CARAMEL TRUFFLES

Sea salt milk chocolate is one of Rococo's signature Artisan bars, and we have built on the collection by introducing this truffle. It is extremely popular, and this is the sought-after recipe. Stir a little freshly ground black pepper into the finished ganache if you are feeling adventurous; it works well.

Makes approximately 60 truffles

Special equipment
18 x 18cm stainless steel frame

Ingredients
280g Valrhona Caramelia chocolate (see p249 for stockists), broken into pieces
20g cocoa butter (see p249 for stockists), chopped
100ml whipping cream
A pinch of Fleur de Sel salt (we use Halen Môn from Anglesey)
40g liquid glucose or honey
45g softened unsalted butter, diced 500g good quality milk or dark chocolate, tempered (see p226–228), for chablon and dipping
Lots of cocoa powder, to finish

Make a chablon base (see page 229) with the tempered chocolate, and place the frame on top of the chablon before it sets.

Melt the Caramelia chocolate and cocoa butter in a bowl over a bain-marie, and set it aside.

Place the cream, salt and glucose or honey in a small heavy-based saucepan and gently heat until it is almost boiling. Stir about a third of the hot cream into the melted chocolate with a rubber spatula. As the mixture starts to thicken, stir in the next third, and by the addition of the final third you will have a smooth and glossy ganache. Beat the butter into the emulsion, or blend it in with a stick blender, until it has been fully incorporated.

Pour the ganache mixture into the frame set on top of the chablon, spread it out evenly and store it in a cool, dry place (maximum 18°C) or at room temperature, ideally overnight, to firm up to a butter-like consistency.

Remove the frame and cut the ganache into 3.5cm x 1.5cm rectangles. Dip the rectangles one by one in the tempered chocolate, using a dipping fork. Place them in a rectangular container with enough cocoa powder to bury the truffles. Leave them to set and turn over once as they are setting. After 2–3 minutes, when you can feel they have set, scoop them out into a sieve and shake off the excess cocoa powder.

The truffles will keep well for up to a week if covered in tempered chocolate and kept in a cool, dry place.

HAZELNUT PRALINE PASTE

Praline is a paste of almonds or hazelnuts, or a mixture of both, and caramelised sugar. You can also use walnuts or pecan nuts. Buy the freshest nuts you can get your hands on — old nuts can taste rancid and bitter because the oils oxidise very quickly. This praline adds a beautiful crunch to Donna Tella da Kids (see page 117) and Hazelnut Praline Rochers (see page 48).

Ingredients

200g skinned hazelnuts/almonds

150g granulated sugar

Preheat the oven to 150°C/gas mark 2. Spread the nuts out evenly on a large non-stick baking sheet and roast for 10–15 minutes until light golden brown. Remove the tray from the oven and keep the nuts in a warm place. Place a clean and grease-free heavy-based saucepan over a medium heat. Once hot, put a third of the sugar in the pan. Heat the sugar, shaking the pan regularly, and stir until the sugar melts. Add another third of the sugar to the pan and let it melt, stirring with a wooden spoon, then finally add the remaining third. Once all the sugar is in the pan and caramelising, the temperature will rise quite quickly and the sugar will turn a dark brown caramel colour. Tip the warm roasted nuts into the caramel, stirring quickly to coat all nuts. Pour the caramelised nuts on to a baking tray lined with a silicone mat or oiled greaseproof paper and leave them to cool.

When the nuts have cooled completely, place them in a plastic bag and smash them into small pieces with a rolling pin, then transfer the pieces to the bowl of a food processor or Thermomix. Blitz it to a smooth paste. Be patient, as this will take some time: at first it will turn into a powder, then into a rough paste, and eventually into a fine paste, as the oil in the nuts is released by the increased temperature of the mixture. If you are using a food processor, after a few minutes pause the blitzing to scrape down the paste and to give the motor a chance to cool down.

To make a crunchy praline, keep back a quarter of the caramelised nuts once they've been roughly blitzed. Process the remaining nuts to a paste as before and then stir in the roughly blitzed nuts to give the praline some texture. The praline paste can be stored in an airtight container for up to 1 month. The oils will separate if left to stand for a few weeks. This is normal, just stir it all together again.

HAZELNUT PRALINE ROCHERS

A Rococo classic – light, crunchy and nutty – and best when they are freshly made. You can use almonds instead of hazelnuts, if you wish: follow the Hazelnut Praline Paste recipe but substitute almonds for the hazelnuts, use tempered milk chocolate for dipping, and finish them with nibbed almonds.

Makes 80 rochers

Special equipment
Probe thermometer

18 x 18cm stainless steel frame

Ingredients
1 quantity Hazelnut Praline Paste (see p46)

150g Caramelia chocolate, or 135g milk chocolate couverture (35% cocoa solids)

20g crushed crêpe dentelles, rice crispies or puffed rice

500g good quality dark chocolate, tempered (see p226–228), for chablon and dipping

120g roasted nibbed hazelnuts, to decorate

Melt the praline paste and Caramelia chocolate in a bowl over a bain-marie until it reaches 45°C, then pour it on to a marble slab. Temper the mixture using the tablier method (see page 227), bringing the temperature down to 25°C. If you don't have a marble slab, sit the bowl in a larger bowl of iced water and stir the mixture continuously until it reaches 25°C, being careful not to let any water get into the chocolate. Scrape the praline chocolate mixture (if you used the marble slab tempering method) from the marble block back into the bowl and stir in the crêpe dentelles. Pour the mixture on to a non-stick mat or sheet of silicone on a baking tray and spread out evenly. Put the tray in a cool, dry place for 1 hour to set.

Make a chablon base (see page 229) with the tempered chocolate, and place the frame on top of the chablon before it sets.

Cut the set praline chocolate into small pieces and place into the mixing bowl of a free-standing food mixer fitted with the paddle attachment, and beat until mixture is aerated, soft and fluffy. Spoon the mixture into the frame set on top of the chablon, spread it out evenly with a stepped palette knife and store it in a cool, dry place (maximum 18°C) or at room temperature, ideally overnight, to firm up to a butter-like consistency. Roast the hazelnuts and allow to go cold.

Remove the frame and cut the praline into roughly 2cm cubes. Dip the cubes one by one in the tempered chocolate, using a dipping fork. Place them on a baking tray lined with a silicone mat or greaseproof paper, and sprinkle each rocher with the nibbed hazelnuts. Leave the rochers to set, then coat them a second time in the tempered chocolate to completely cover the nuts. The rochers will keep well for up to 2 weeks if covered in tempered chocolate and kept in a cool, dry place.

GIANDUJA PRALINE

This is a very smooth Italian-style praline paste pronounced 'gee-an-doo-ya'. It can be placed in chocolate cases, or used to fill hen's eggs (see page 132).

Makes 60–70 chocolates

Special equipment
Chocolate cups (see p249
for stockists)
Probe thermometer
Disposable piping bag

Ingredients
250g whole skinned hazelnuts
100g good quality milk chocolate
(40% cocoa solids), broken
into pieces
30g cocoa butter (see p249
for stockists), chopped
250g icing sugar
Whole pistachios or Orange
Powder (see p94), to decorate

Preheat the oven to 150°C/gas mark 2.

Spread the nuts out evenly on a large non-stick baking sheet and roast for 10–15 minutes until light golden brown. Meanwhile, gently melt the chocolate and cocoa butter in a bowl over a bain-marie, or in a microwave (see page 223) until it reaches 40–45°C.

Remove the hazelnuts from the oven and tip them into a food processor. Add the icing sugar and blitz them together for about 5 minutes, stopping the machine and loosening the mixture from the sides of the bowl every now and then, until the oils are released from the nuts and they form a smooth paste. You might also need to stop the machine every now and then if it seems like it might be overheating.

Add the melted chocolate and cocoa butter to the hazelnut paste, blitz again to combine, then transfer the mixture to a bowl. Temper the mixture using the tablier method (see page 227), and let the mixture cool down to 25–26°C. Place the gianduja into a disposable piping bag and pipe it into chocolate cups or chocolate-lined moulds. Decorate each chocolate with a nibbed pistachio or a pinch of Orange Powder. Store in an airtight container. The chocolates will keep for up to 2 weeks.

Variation: Orange praline
Mix 2 teaspoons of Orange Powder (see page 94), or a few drops of organic orange oil, into the praline before piping.

CON—
FEC—
TION—
ERY

MARZIPAN

These are two very simple marzipan recipes. I came up with the idea for Cherry and Walnut Marzipan when I rediscovered a jar of cherries that had been soaking in brandy for years. The Seville Orange and Whisky Marzipan is best made (in my opinion) with dark bitter marmalade and a peaty malt whisky, such as an Islay. If you prefer to omit the alcohol, you can use a little orange-flower water and fresh orange juice instead, or try swapping the cherries for other preserved fruits such as pears in brandy or prunes in rum. Really, these flavoured marzipans are moveable feasts – I beg you to experiment.

Each makes approximately
40 pieces

Ingredients

200g blanched almonds
100g shelled walnuts
100g icing sugar
50g pitted cherries in brandy, stones removed and brandy squeezed out
Unsweetened cocoa powder, for dusting (optional)
500g good quality dark chocolate, tempered (see p226–228), for dipping (optional)

Cherry and walnut marzipan

Blitz the almonds and walnuts in short pulses in a food processor until roughly ground. Add the sugar and blitz once more until finely ground. Add the cherries and pulse to make a smooth, moist dough (add a teaspoon of the brandy from the jar of cherries, if necessary). Shape the marzipan into roughly 10g balls. Place them on a plate or tray and leave them to dry for 1 hour, then dust the balls with cocoa powder, or dip them into tempered chocolate and leave them to set. Alternatively, if you have small metal petit fours moulds, dust them with icing sugar before pressing the marzipan into them. Remove them when firm and place in paper cases. Eat within a couple of days.

Ingredients

300g blanched almonds
50g icing sugar
75g marmalade
3–4 tbsp whisky

Seville orange and whisky marzipan

Blitz the almonds in short pulses in a food processor until roughly ground. Add the icing sugar and blitz once more until finely ground. Add the marmalade and whisky and pulse to make a smooth, moist dough. Shape the marzipan into roughly 10g balls, leave to dry for 1 hour, then roll them in cocoa powder or dip them in tempered chocolate and leave them to set.

DOLCETTI DI PASTAREALE DI CASA SERRILLI

My dear friend Cristina has been kind enough to share her secret marzipan recipe, passed to her by her Italian aunt, as it had been passed to her by successive generations of the Serrilli family. The recipe hails from Sicily yet offers more than a passing glance at the Middle East. This is food made with love, and it is perfect for sharing. Make the marzipan just before you need it, as it dries out quickly, or freeze it. Serve the stuffed fruits and nuts with a shot of espresso, limoncello or noccino.

Makes 100 pieces

Ingredients

200g shelled pistachios

75g blanched almonds

180g icing sugar, plus extra for dusting

1 tsp gin

1 tsp orange flower water or rose water

1 large egg white, lightly beaten with a fork to just break it up

Dried apricots, dates, prunes, halved figs and walnut halves (100 pieces in total)

Unsweetened cocoa powder, for dusting (optional)

500g good quality dark chocolate, tempered (see p226–228), for dipping (optional)

Blitz the almonds and pistachios in short pulses in the bowl of a food processor until ground quite fine. Add the icing sugar and blitz again until very finely ground into a powder. Add the gin and flower water, and pulse to combine. With the machine still running on pulse, gradually add the egg white until the mixture just sticks together in clumps (you may not need it all). Transfer the paste to a clean work surface dusted with icing sugar and knead until smooth. Roll it into a long sausage and cut it into 4–5g pieces to form 100 small balls.

The dried apricots, dates and prunes should have a small opening where the stone has been taken out: gently push the balls of marzipan through the holes into the cavity. Stuff the marzipan into the halved figs, and knead it into the undersides of the walnuts and squash two together to make a sandwich. If you have any marzipan left over, you can freeze it. To use again, defrost, grate and restore to a paste with a little gin or flower water.

Dust the stuffed fruits and nuts with cocoa powder, or dip them into tempered chocolate to make indulgent 'bouchées', and place them on a sheet of baking parchment to set. Store the dolcetti in an airtight container, and eat within 1 week.

HONEYCOMB CRUNCH

As an urban beekeeper I find cinder toffee (also known as honeycomb) is a lovely way for me to share my honey. Enrobing it in dark chocolate tempers its sweetness: go for unsweetened 100% cocoa solids, an 80% variety, 70% or milk chocolate – the choice is yours.

Makes 30–40 generous chunks

Special equipment

20 x 30cm shallow rectangular cake tin

Probe thermometer

Ingredients

200g honey

100g liquid glucose

400g golden caster sugar

100ml water

20ml cider vinegar

10g bicarbonate of soda

500g good quality dark chocolate, tempered (see p226–228), for dipping (optional)

Line the cake tin with silicone paper, non-stick baking paper or generously oiled greaseproof paper.

Put the honey, glucose, sugar, water and vinegar in a deep heavy-based saucepan (a preserving pan is ideal) and heat slowly until the sugar has dissolved, then bring the mixture to the boil and let it bubble away until the thermometer reads 145–150°C or 'hard crack' and is a rich golden caramel colour. You need to watch it like a hawk, as the temperature will suddenly shoot up. Turn off the heat immediately. Sift the bicarbonate of soda over the toffee and stir it quickly and thoroughly with a wooden spoon (it will bubble up furiously), then pour the mixture into the prepared tray and leave it to cool. When it has set, take it out of the tray and break it up into chunks with a sharp knife.

Dip each chunk in tempered chocolate, if desired, within an hour of making the honeycomb and place on a sheet of baking parchment to set. This will stop them from going sticky.

Keep in an airtight container and eat as quickly as possible.

CHOCOLATE DIPPED CANDIED PEEL

This method of candying makes the peel almost transparent and particularly creamy with a gentle and elegant flavour. Use the stock syrup as a base for cordials and cocktails, or drizzle it over cake.

Ingredients

2kg unwaxed organic pink or white grapefruit, oranges or lemons

1 litre water

1kg caster sugar

500g good quality dark chocolate, tempered (see p226–228), for dipping (optional)

Wash and brush the fruit under running water. Using a sharp knife, score around the fruit from top to bottom, cutting the skin into quarters, without cutting into the fruit. The cut should be the depth of the zest and the pith. Peel the skin away from the fruit with your fingers, lifting it away in its quarters; you want to keep the pith with the peel because this forms the soft body of the candied fruit.

To speed things up, fill two large saucepans with water, and bring them to boil. Add the peel to one of the two pans and simmer for 10 minutes. Drain, and place the peel in the second pan, and simmer for 10 minutes. Meanwhile, refill the first pan with water and bring it to a boil. Drain and place the peel back in the refilled first pan and simmer for 10 minutes. Refill the second pan of boiling water, repeating the process with the peel – twice more for grapefruit and lemons, once more for oranges – to remove as much bitterness as possible.

After the final draining, refill the saucepan with 1 litre of water, add the peel and 250g of the sugar, and bring it back to a gentle simmer for 15 minutes. Add another 250g of the sugar and simmer for another 15 minutes. Continue adding 250g of sugar every 15 minutes until all the sugar has been added. Remove the pan from the heat and leave to cool, then carefully decant the peel into sterilised jars with the syrup. The peel will keep well for a couple of months in sealed jars, stored in the fridge.

When needed, drain to remove excess syrup and dry on kitchen paper. Cut the peel into strips, spreading out on a wire rack covered with a sheet of non-stick baking paper. Place the rack in a warm place and leave the peel to dry out for at least 48 hours, or place it in a 50°C/gas ¼ oven (as low as it will go) for a couple of hours. Dip the dry peel in tempered chocolate, if desired, and place on a sheet of baking parchment to set. Store in a cool, dry place and eat within 1 or 2 weeks.

CHOCOLATE AND WALNUT FUDGE

I used to make Monsieur Bon-Bon's Secret 'Fooj' with my sister Ros when we were children, though the recipe used condensed milk and cocoa powder, which I now find far too sweet, so I have given the recipe an adult makeover.

Makes 36–42 pieces

Special equipment

18cm square shallow baking tin, or silicone mould

Probe thermometer

Ingredients

Grape seed oil, for greasing

450g caster sugar

150ml milk

A pinch of sea salt

50g honey, golden syrup, or glucose

150g unsalted butter, diced

1 tsp vanilla extract

85g walnut halves, fresh if possible, broken into small pieces. (Buy them in season if possible, and shell them yourself. They don't keep well shelled.)

100g good quality dark chocolate (70% cocoa solids), roughly chopped

Lightly oil the tin, then base-line with non-stick baking paper. Part-fill your sink with cold water.

Place the sugar, milk, salt, honey, butter and vanilla extract in a heavy-based deep saucepan and heat gently, stirring now and then, to dissolve the sugar. Bring to the boil without stirring and cook for about 15 minutes, until the temperature reaches 116°C and keep it at this temperature for 2 minutes. After this, immediately take the pan off the heat and plunge the base briefly in the cold water to stop the boiling. Remove from the water, stir in the walnuts and chocolate and leave on a cool surface for 5 minutes. Stir the mixture very briefly until it starts to show signs of thickening and loses its gloss (this prevents sugar crystals forming), then quickly pour into the prepared tin. Mark the fudge into 2.5–3cm squares and leave it to set before cutting and removing from the tin.

It will store for up to 2 weeks in an airtight container.

CHOCOLATE SALAMI

This chocolate 'saucisson' falls somewhere between a ganache and rocky road, and can be adapted endlessly to suit your taste and the ingredients you have to hand. You can spice it up with chilli flakes, add whole pine nuts, use dark or milk chocolate, or add dried fruits such as raisins and cranberries. It makes a perfect gift for Christmas or any other time, and you can have fun making a customised paper sleeve for it.

Makes one long sausage or several smaller ones

Special equipment
Sushi mat (optional)

Ingredients
250g good quality dark chocolate (62% cocoa solids)
190ml whipping cream
25g liquid glucose or honey
50g softened unsalted butter, cut into small pieces
75g almond biscotti, broken into walnut-half-sized pieces
150g lightly toasted nuts (almonds and hazelnuts) or shelled un-toasted pistachios, some left whole and some very roughly chopped
1 tbsp of your favourite spirit eg. whisky, brandy, or rum (optional)
50g icing sugar, to dust

Melt the chocolate in a large bowl over a bain-marie.

Pour the cream and glucose or honey into a heavy-based saucepan and heat to boiling point, then remove from the heat. Slowly pour the cream and glucose mixture on to the melted chocolate, incorporating it with a rubber spatula until the mixture is smooth and glossy. Beat the butter into the ganache, or blend it in with a stick blender. Stir in the biscotti, nuts and alcohol (if using), cover and chill for a couple of hours until it is firm but malleable.

Remove the ganache from the bowl, place it on a large sheet of clingfilm and roll it into a 6–7cm thick roll (within the clingfilm). Wrap it tightly in a sushi mat if you have one, to mark the surface of the roll with ridges. Chill the sausage-shaped ganache for a couple of hours until it is firm enough to slice, but not rock hard. Unwrap, and roll the 'sausage' in icing sugar, to give it that 'salt cured' salami look. Secure it with string at both ends, or tie it with a butcher's knot to mimic a classic saucisson, and chill for a couple of hours before serving. To serve, slice into rounds.

VANILLA MARSHMALLOWS

I first experienced guimauves when our last chocolatier Laurent Couchaux made them at our Motcomb Street shop. They were a revelation, worlds apart from the commercially produced marshmallows I ate as a child. They keep well and make a fantastic present. For a pretty finish, dip them in Rainbow Sugar (see page 92) or tempered chocolate.

Makes approximately 54 pieces

Special equipment
21 x 30 x 5cm shallow,
rectangular cake or brownie tin
Sugar thermometer

Ingredients
Flavourless oil such as grape seed,
for greasing
50g cornflour, for dusting
50g icing sugar, for dusting
For the syrup
140g liquid glucose
400g caster sugar
150ml cold water
For the marshmallow mixture
175ml cold water
38g leaf gelatine
200g liquid glucose
Seeds scraped from 2 large
vanilla pods

Lightly oil the cake or brownie tin and line it with a large sheet of clingfilm pushing it into all the corners. Generously oil the clingfilm with more oil to ensure the marshmallows don't get stuck.

For the syrup, put the liquid glucose, caster sugar and water into a small heavy-based saucepan (make sure it is completely clean and free of fat) and warm it over a low heat until the sugar has dissolved and the liquid is clear. Make sure it doesn't boil until the sugar has fully dissolved. Meanwhile, put 115ml of the cold water for the marshmallows into a small shallow dish, add the gelatine, one leaf at a time, making sure they are submerged, and leave them to soak for 5 minutes, turning them over halfway through if necessary so that they soak evenly.

Put the remaining water and 200g liquid glucose for the marshmallow mixture into the lightly warmed bowl of a free-standing food mixer fitted with the balloon whisk attachment. Increase the heat under the syrup and boil it rapidly until it reaches 114°C. Don't be tempted to stir the syrup. If any sugar crystals have stuck to the sides of the pan once the syrup is boiling, brush the inside sides of the pan with a pastry brush and cold water. If the stray crystals end up in your syrup, they can cause it to crystallise. When it has almost reached the right temperature, gently melt the gelatine (in a microwave or in a small pan), making sure that it doesn't get any hotter than 60°C. When the syrup reaches 114°C, add it to the bowl and mix on low speed for a few seconds. Add the melted gelatine and vanilla seeds to the bowl. Mix again on low speed, then increase the speed to high and mix for approximately 5 minutes. The mixture will quadruple in volume and become thick, white and fluffy. When it has cooled to 45°C, quickly scrape the mixture into the prepared tin and spread it out into an even layer. Press another sheet of well-oiled clingfilm on to the surface and leave it to set and go cold – approximately 2 hours or overnight. If you want your sugar thermometer to last for many years, let it cool on greaseproof paper and then immerse it in hot water so the sugar can dissolve away before you wash it.

Sift the cornflour and icing sugar into a shallow tray or bowl. Remove the sheet of clingfilm from the surface of the marshmallows and turn it out on to a dusted chopping board. Cut it into 3cm cubes and toss them in the powder to cover all sides, then store in an airtight container for up to 2 weeks.

RASPBERRY MARSHMALLOWS

Vastly different from fluffy industrial pink marshmallows, the beautiful intense pink colour in these special guimauves *comes from using real fruit purée, which gives them a sharp fruit flavour and little chewy bits that cut through the sweetness. Experiment with unsweetened strawberry, blackcurrant, blueberry or passion fruit purée in place of the raspberry.*

Makes approximately 54 pieces

Special equipment
21 x 30 x 5cm shallow,
rectangular cake or brownie tin
Sugar thermometer

Ingredients
Flavourless oil such as grape seed,
for greasing
50g cornflour, for dusting
50g icing sugar, for dusting
For the raspberry syrup
170g liquid glucose
400g caster sugar
110g raspberry purée (blitz
fresh raspberries and sieve
them to remove the pips, or
use shop-bought frozen purée
(see p249 for stockists)
For the marshmallow mixture
115ml cold water
38g leaf gelatine
170g liquid glucose
110g raspberry purée (as above)
30g freeze-dried raspberry pieces
(see p249 for stockists)

Lightly oil the cake or brownie tin and line it with a large sheet of clingfilm, pushing it into all the corners. Generously oil the clingfilm with more oil. For the raspberry syrup, put the liquid glucose, caster sugar and raspberry purée into a heavy-based saucepan and warm it over a low heat until the sugar has dissolved. In the meantime, put the water for the marshmallows into a small shallow dish, add the gelatine leaves one at a time, making sure they are submerged, and leave them to soak for 5 minutes, turning them over halfway through so that they soak evenly.

Put the remaining liquid glucose and raspberry purée for the marshmallow mixture into the lightly warmed bowl of a free-standing food mixer fitted with the balloon whisk attachment. Increase the heat under the raspberry syrup and boil it rapidly until it reaches 114°C. Gently melt the leaf gelatine (in a microwave or small pan), making sure that it doesn't get any hotter than 60°C. When the syrup reaches 114°C, add it to the mixer bowl and mix on low speed for a few seconds. Add the melted gelatine to the bowl. Mix again on low speed, then increase the speed to high for approximately 5 minutes. The mixture will quadruple in volume and become thick, pink and fluffy. When it has cooled to 45°C, add the freeze-dried raspberry pieces and mix well. Quickly scrape the mixture into the prepared tin and spread it out evenly. Press another sheet of well-oiled clingfilm on to the surface and leave it to set and go cold – approximately 2 hours or overnight.

Sift the cornflour and icing sugar into a shallow tray or bowl. Remove the sheet of clingfilm from the surface of the marshmallow and turn it out on to a dusted chopping board. Cut it into 3cm cubes and toss them in the powder to cover all sides, then store in an airtight container for up to 2 weeks.

DECO—
RATING
CHOC—
OLATE

PAINTING & MOULDING: HEARTS & FISH

We have been handpainting our chocolate eggs, fish and animals for over 20 years and each one really is a work of art, individually made to express the quirky nature of Rococo. These hearts and fish are great fun to make. The secret is to do everything backwards, starting with the patterns or colours that you see on the surface of the finished chocolate.

Makes 8 hearts

Special equipment
8 heart moulds (see p249 for stockists)
Stepped spatula
Small paintbrushes
Disposable piping bag

Ingredients
20g good quality white chocolate, tempered (see p226–228)
500g good quality dark chocolate, tempered (see p226–228)

Clean the heart mould thoroughly, polishing it with cotton wool to make the surface as shiny as possible. Prepare a piping bag: cut out a large square of baking paper, and fold one corner up to make a triangle. Press your finger on the crease, fold the triangle again so that the section you folded over is halved. Roll the triangle into a cone shape, folding the top outwards over the edge of the roll to secure it (or use tape to be sure). Fill it halfway with tempered white chocolate and fold down the top of the bag pressing the chocolate down to the tip. Snip off the tip of the bag to make a tiny opening, about as big as the top of a ball-point pen, and gently squeeze to create patterns on the inside of the mould. Leave to set for a few minutes in a cool place. Using a small paintbrush, brush a thin layer of tempered dark chocolate over the white chocolate. Fill the moulds with the tempered dark chocolate, tap the edge of the mould with the handle of the wooden spoon to release any air bubbles, then smooth them over with a stepped spatula. Leave to set for a few hours in a cool place, so that the tempered chocolate crystallises, giving your hearts a shiny smooth surface. When the chocolate is set, flex the mould gently and in one action turn the mould over and tap the long edge of it on the table. Your hearts should drop out of the moulds with ease.

Variation: Chocolate fish

You need a 5-sardine mould, coloured cocoa butter (see page 248 for stockists), and tempered white and dark chocolate (as above). Carefully pipe little dots of tempered dark chocolate into the moulds for the fish eyes. Brush the fish tails and fins with tempered dark chocolate, and the body of the fish with coloured cocoa butter and tempered white chocolate. Fill the moulds with tempered dark chocolate and put aside to set.

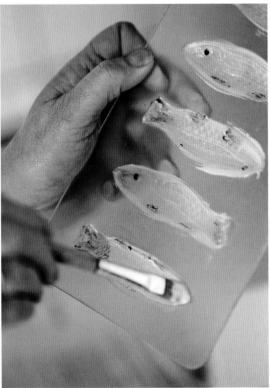

WRITING WITH CHOCOLATE

Writing a message in chocolate adds a wonderful personal touch to a celebration cake. The golden rule is: remember you need to use mirror writing. Work quickly and confidently, and experiment with methods of applying chocolate to the acetate: a brush, your fingers, a piping bag or even a spray gun produce equally attractive results.

Special equipment

Black marker pen

Paintbrush

Sheet of acetate

Ingredients

200g good quality dark chocolate, tempered (see p226–228)

50g good quality white chocolate, tempered (see p226–228)

Write your message on a sheet of greaseproof paper with a black marker pen or a pencil. Turn the paper over (placing it on top of a white sheet of paper if necessary, so that you can see the text as mirror writing) and place a sheet of acetate over it. Half fill a paper piping bag (see page 74) with tempered white chocolate, snip the end, and carefully trace the message on to the acetate. Leave it to set for a couple of minutes, then swiftly brush over the writing with tempered dark chocolate and then put a layer of the dark chocolate over to cover all the writing. Make sure the layer is thick enough so it will not be too fragile when it's finished; it needs to be at least 2–3mm. Leave it to set again for a couple of minutes, then place another sheet of acetate on top of the writing, followed by a baking tray to weigh it down. Leave it to set for 1 hour.

SPRAY TAN
TEDDY BEARS

This method unravels how to create a furry or flocked effect to embellish the surface of tempered chocolate – great for bunnies, cats, bears – or anything you want. You can play a little by masking off areas if you want to get super creative – you could even make little costumes that you peel off to get tan lines! We have seen Heston Blumenthal manipulating chocolate using thermal effects, though in the opposite way – he sprayed chocolate with liquid coolants to create a pliable chocolate. The principal behind this technique is thermal shock, using very cold chocolate and spraying with fluid warm chocolate and extra cocoa butter. It's a little bit of a challenge, but great fun – you do need a spray gun and tempered chocolate to start with.

Special equipment

Small bear chocolate mould
(see p249 for stockists)

Small paint gun

Probe thermometer

Ingredients

250g good quality dark, milk
or white tempered chocolate
(see p226–228)

For the dark chocolate spray mix

350g good quality dark chocolate
(70% cocoa solids)

150g cocoa butter

For the milk chocolate spray mix

300g good quality milk chocolate
(40% cocoa solids)

200g cocoa butter

For the white chocolate spray mix

350g good quality white chocolate

150g cocoa butter

Make the moulded chocolate bears with the tempered chocolate shade (dark, milk or white) of your choice, following the method from Hearts & Fish on page 74. Once removed from the moulds, using a warm stainless steel tray, rub the flat sides of the teddy bears to melt the edges and neatly stick them together. Chill them for 30 minutes or place them in the freezer for 10 minutes.

The paint gun should be warmed gently in the oven at the lowest setting, with the door open and the cord cable and plug left outside the oven. Meanwhile melt a contrasting shade of chocolate (dark, milk or white) and the cocoa butter together in a bowl over a bain-marie, until it reaches 40–45°C. Pass it through a sieve into a heat proof jug. Fill the reservoir of the paint gun with the melted chocolate and cocoa butter mixture. Take your chilled bears out of the fridge, and spray immediately on all sides. Leave at room temperature to set. They will keep for well over a month, if stored in a cool, dry place.

DECORATING WITH COCOA BUTTER TRANSFERS

We use quite a few patterned transfers on our Rococo Couture ganache collection chocolates. They are acetate sheets embossed with cocoa butter and edible pigments, and you can buy them pre-printed from specialist stockists (see page 248).

Cut the transfer sheet into squares, a little larger than the dimensions of the chocolates you are making. After dipping your ganache in tempered chocolate and placing it on a baking tray lined with silicone paper, carefully place a piece of transfer sheet, pattern-side down, on to the surface of the chocolate (you need to do this quickly, before the chocolate starts setting). Smooth down gently to make sure there is a good contact between the transfer and the chocolate. Leave the chocolates to set for 2–3 hours at room temperature before peeling off the transfer sheets. The longer the transfer sheet is left on the chocolate, the shinier the finished chocolate.

You can also use pattern transfers to decorate thin shards of tempered chocolate for decorating cakes, pastries or desserts, much like we do to make the base for the Choc-en-bouche (see page 140). Place the transfer sheet pattern-side up on a flat surface, and spread a 2mm-thick layer of tempered chocolate over the sheet with a stepped palette knife. If you want a neat shape or piece of chocolate, use a small paring knife to cut the chocolate before it sets, otherwise you can break it into shards after it has set. Leave the sheet of chocolate in a cool place for a couple of hours. You will need to cover with a layer of clingfilm and weigh down the sheets (a heavy baking tray will do) to keep them from curling up as the tempered chocolate sets.

CHOCOLATE CIGARS

These can be made with the classic ganache recipe, infused with a touch of Lapsang Souchong to give a slightly smoky flavour. The inspiration came from Luke Frost, Head Pastry Chef at Simon Radley's Michelin-starred restaurant at the Chester Grosvenor, where we have just opened our 4th store. They are served with coffee after dinner from a humidor.

Makes 16 cigars

Special equipment
Disposable piping bag fitted with
15mm round nozzle
Two large fresh leaves, washed
and dried (such as Cocoa if you
can find them or Hydrangea),
for rolling

Ingredients
1 quantity Classic Truffle ganache
(see p26)
1 tsp loose Lapsang Souchong
tea leaves, plus extra for dipping
(optional)
20g crushed crêpe dentelles (see
p249 for stockists) or cornflakes
Unsweetened cocoa powder,
for dusting

Make the Classic Truffle ganache, following the method on page 26, but infuse the cream with the Lapsang Souchong tea leaves for 3 minutes. Pass the cream through a sieve into a heatproof measuring jug to get rid of the leaves, topping the cream up with more cream to 200ml if you need to, before pouring it over the melted chocolate. Pour the ganache into a plastic container and place clingfilm on the surface. Leave it to cool for an hour or two and until it reaches piping consistency.

Spoon the ganache into the disposable piping bag fitted with the 15mm nozzle. Pipe 6 x 30cm lengths of ganache on to a large baking tray lined with a silicone mat or greaseproof paper. Set aside on a cool, dry place (maximum 18°C) or at room temperature, ideally overnight, to firm up to a butter-like consistency.

Cut each length in half to make 12 x 15cm-long cigars. Roll one end in your fingers to give it a tapered shape, then roll them in cocoa powder. To get the tobacco leaf effect, roll the cocoa-dusted cigars, one by one, between two large leaves, lightly pressing the pronounced veins of the leaves to make impressions on the cigar. Be careful when handling the cigars because they are quite fragile. If you like, make paper sleeves from tissue paper, folding 12 x 8cm squares into 4 to make a 2cm-wide band, wrapping them around the cigars and securing them with a little sticky tape. Cut the blunt ends of each cigar with a hot knife and dip each end into a bowl of crushed dentelles or cornflakes. You can even add a few leaves of ground Lapsang Souchong to the crushed dentelles or cornflakes, to give a 'chopped tobacco' effect. The cigars keep for a day or two, and make a perfect gift: Use an old cigar box for presentation (you may need to adjust the size and length of the cigar to fit).

CRYSTALLISED ROSE PETALS

These add a beautiful finishing touch to chocolates or cakes. Use smaller petals, or crushed petals, to decorate chocolates.

Ingredients

20 unblemished fragrant rose petals (make sure they have not been sprayed with pesticide)

1 medium egg white

100g caster sugar

Make sure that the petals are washed and completely dry. Beat the egg white briefly (you don't want it to be frothy) and place it in one bowl, and the sugar in another.

Using a paint brush or pastry brush, carefully paint both sides of each petal with egg white, then dip them in the sugar so that they are completely covered. Place the petals on a baking tray lined with non-stick baking paper and leave them in a warm, dry place to dry overnight. Leave them longer if you can, up to two days, to ensure they are completely dry and brittle before you store them. The dry crystallised petals can be kept for a week or two in an airtight container.

WHITE CHOCOLATE 'SOIL'

This recipe is one of those accidental discoveries. I was melting white chocolate and forgot about it; it got too hot. The result was a wonderful sweet caramelised crunchy 'soil', which we use to decorate chocolate mousse served in flowerpots or to sprinkle on dipped truffles. Rumour has it that this happy accident was also how Valrhona's Caramelia chocolate came about.

Ingredients

140–200g Valrhona Ivoire white chocolate, broken into pieces

You may want to make a larger quantity depending on what you are using it for.

Heat the oven to 130°C/gas mark 1. Place the chocolate on a tray lined with a silicone mat or non-stick baking paper and bake for 15 minutes, by which time it should have gone slightly hard and started to go brown. Break up the chocolate into coarse crumbs with the back of a fork. Return to the oven and continue to cook for 45–50 minutes, stirring it frequently now and then to separate the crumbs and achieve an even texture. At first it looks like clotted cream, then it solidifies and starts to brown. Remove it from the oven when the chocolate looks and feels like deeply golden sandy breadcrumbs. Leave to cool. It keeps well for at least 2 weeks in an airtight container, if you can resist nibbling at it.

RAINBOW SUGAR

This coloured sugar is fun to make, and a great activity for children. Pink sugar looks like crumbled crystallised rose petals, and red sugar mixed with poppy seeds gives a very dramatic finish to truffles. You can also roll Marshmallows (see page 68) in it, or use it to decorate Floral Cream Fondants (see page 43). Try experimenting with pure colour and no alcohol for a vivid effect.

Ingredients

100g granulated sugar

2–3 tbsp vodka or gin (37–80% alcohol; the higher the alcohol content, the better the results)

A few drops of water-based food colouring, depending on its strength (colour of your choice)

Place the sugar in a bowl. Mix the vodka or gin with the food colouring in a little eggcup, until the colour is evenly distributed, and pour it over the sugar to wet it. Work the coloured alcohol around the sugar with the end of a teaspoon, then spread out the coloured sugar on a large baking tray covered with a sheet of silicone paper or greaseproof paper. Leave it somewhere warm for 2 hours (a very low oven works well), stirring occasionally, until the sugar is completely dry. Or let it dry naturally in a small container for a couple of days, stirring it once or twice a day. Once the sugar is completely dry, store it in an airtight container and it will keep for a couple of months. If you find it has set in a lump, run a rolling pin over it to separate the grains of sugar again.

Variation: Fruit sugar

Another way of making pretty coloured sugar is to mix icing sugar with crushed freeze-dried fruit, such as raspberries, blueberries or blackcurrants. Mix 5g of crushed fruit with 100g icing sugar, and use as rainbow sugar to decorate chocolates, sweets or cakes, such as Champagne Truffles (see page 36).

ORANGE POWDER

We use this as a chocolate decoration, but it is also perfect for perking up a ganache or dressing up a dessert. Use Seville oranges if you want an intense and bitter flavour; lemon, lime and grapefruit also work well using the same technique. Save the orange-flavoured syrup – it's great for serving with desserts, or place a teaspoon of syrup in the bottom of a champagne flute and top up with sparkling wine or Champagne.

Ingredients

2 large organic, unwaxed oranges, scrubbed under running water

200ml water

200g caster sugar

Peel the zest from the oranges with a small sharp knife, taking care to remove as little of the bitter white pith as possible, and cut it into thin strips. Place the water and sugar in a small heavy-based saucepan and gently heat until the sugar has dissolved. Bring to the boil and simmer for 2 minutes, then add the peel to the syrup and let it poach over a low heat for 2 minutes. Carefully remove the peel from the syrup with a pair of tongs or slotted metal spoon, drain on a clean dry cloth, pat dry and place the pieces on a silicone mat or baking tray lined with baking parchment. Bake in the oven at 90–100°C/gas mark ¼ (as low as possible) for an hour, and then keep the oven door ajar for a further hour or two until the strips of peel are completely dry. Allow to cool. Blitz the dry peel until finely chopped (not powdered) in a mini food processor or grind it using a mortar and pestle and store in an airtight container for up to 2 weeks.

DES—
SERTS,
SAUCES,
DRINKS
& ICE
CREAMS

CLASSIC CHOCOLATE MOUSSE

Chocolate mousse can be difficult to get right, but a ganache base makes perfect mousse every time. Work quickly when incorporating the mixtures, to avoid the mousse cooling and solidifying.

Serves 12

Ingredients

320g Valrhona Manjari dark chocolate (64% cocoa solids), broken into small pieces

150ml whipping cream

3 eggs, separated, at room temperature

60g caster sugar

Melt the chocolate in a bowl over a bain-marie. Remove the bowl from the heat and set aside.

Pour the whipping cream into a heavy-based saucepan and heat until almost boiling, then remove the pan from the heat and gradually pour the melted chocolate into the pan, incorporating it into the chocolate mixture with a rubber spatula, until mixture is smooth and glossy. Whisk the egg yolks, stir them into the chocolate mixture and set the bowl aside.

In a spotlessly clean bowl beat the egg whites with an electric hand whisk or a free-standing mixer, and whisk at medium speed. As soon as they become frothy, add half the sugar and continue to beat, moving the whisk around the bowl to catch all the mixture. When the mixture reaches soft peaks, add the remaining sugar and continue to beat until it forms soft shiny peaks.

Briskly beat a quarter of the egg whites into the chocolate mixture until fully incorporated. Gently fold in the next quarter of the egg whites with a large metal spoon or rubber spatula, followed by the remaining egg whites. With each addition of egg whites the mousse will get softer and lighter. Spoon or pipe the mousse into individual pots, small glasses or coffee cups, cover, and chill for 1–2 hours until set. Decorate, if you wish, with a Chocolate Lace Biscuit (see page 183), chocolate wafers, whipped cream, fresh fruit or chocolate shavings.

Variation: Boozy mousse

Add the tipple of your fancy at the end of Step 2 with the egg yolks. You will need to adjust the quantity of whipping cream so you still have 150ml liquid in total.

WHIPPED STRAWBERRY MOUSSE

This is a light, deliciously fruity dessert. Make it with dark chocolate instead of milk if you prefer your puddings a little less sweet, or swap the strawberries for raspberries. Here it is served unadulterated, but you could use it to fill the Chocolate Roulade (see page 171).

Serves 6–8

Ingredients

175g Caramelia chocolate (see p248 for stockists), broken into pieces

110g unsweetened strawberry or raspberry purée – make it at home with 200g fresh or frozen fruit, puréed and passed through a fine sieve, to yield 110g, or use Cap Fruit's ready-made version (see p249 for stockists)

25g honey

300ml whipping cream

Melt the Caramelia chocolate in a bowl over a bain-marie. Remove the bowl from the heat and set aside.

Place the fruit purée in a small heavy-based saucepan with the honey and heat gently until almost boiling. Slowly pour the hot fruit mixture on to the melted chocolate, incorporating it with a rubber spatula until the mixture is smooth and glossy. Add the cream to the fruity chocolate mixture, and blend it with a stick blender. Pass the ganache mixture through a fine sieve into a clean bowl. Cover, and chill overnight (it can be made in advance and stored for a couple of days before whipping).

When you are ready to serve, whip the ganache with a whisk (electric or hand-held) until it is the consistency of whipped cream. Spoon or pipe it into individual cups or pots and serve immediately.

WHITE CHOCOLATE MOUSSE

This dessert celebrates one of Rococo's signature flavour combinations: cardamom and saffron. They work beautifully together and counteract the sweetness of the white chocolate. If you don't like saffron or cardamom, replace them with the seeds from half a vanilla pod, scraped into the milk before boiling.

Serves 6

Special equipment
Probe thermometer

Ingredients
140g Rococo Cardamom organic white chocolate or 140g Valrhona Ivoire (or other good quality white chocolate) plus 1–2 cardamom pods, crushed
2 gelatine leaves
A pinch of saffron strands
120ml whole milk
140ml whipping cream
50g shelled and chopped pistachios, to decorate

Melt the chocolate in a bowl over a bain-marie. Remove the bowl from the heat and set aside.

Soak the saffron strands in one tablespoon of the milk, and leave to infuse for 20 minutes. Soften the gelatine leaves in a small bowl of iced water for 10 minutes, then squeeze out excess water. Bring the remaining milk to the boil in a heavy-based saucepan with the crushed cardamom pod (two if you are using plain white chocolate) and the saffron strands. Remove the cardamom pod and take the milk off the heat as soon as it reaches boiling point. Add the softened gelatine to the milk, then blitz with a stick blender to encourage the gelatine to dissolve. Slowly pour the hot milk on to the melted chocolate, incorporating it with a rubber spatula until the mixture is smooth and glossy.

Whip the cream in a large bowl until it forms soft peaks. When the chocolate mixture cools to 35–40°C, gradually fold it into the cream with a rubber spatula until fully incorporated. Pour the mousse into individual pots, small glasses or coffee cups, cover, and chill for 1–2 hours until set. Sprinkle with chopped pistachios just before serving.

LIGHT WHIPPED CREAM & CHOCOLATE MOUSSE

This is a quick and easy egg-free chocolate mousse. Make it with milk or dark chocolate, according to taste. It can be made a day in advance and can also be used to fill the Chocolate Roulade (see page 171).

Serves 6

Special equipment
Probe thermometer

Ingredients
250g good quality milk chocolate (min 35% cocoa solids), broken into small pieces
375ml whipping cream
Fresh fruit, such as blueberries, to decorate (optional)
Chocolate shavings, to decorate (optional)

Melt the chocolate in a bowl over a bain-marie until it reaches 45–50°C. Take care, as milk chocolate has a habit of seizing up when overheated (dark chocolate is more forgiving).

Meanwhile, whip 250ml of the cream in a large bowl until it forms soft peaks. Place the remaining cream in a small heavy-based saucepan and bring it to a gentle simmer. Slowly pour the hot cream on to the melted chocolate, incorporating it with a rubber spatula until the mixture is smooth and glossy (it should be around 45°C). Gently fold in the whipped cream with the spatula. Spoon the mousse into a single serving bowl or small individual glasses. Chill for an hour or two before serving. Decorate, if desired, with fresh fruit, chocolate shavings or more whipped cream.

CRÈME ANGLAISE CHOCOLATE MOUSSE

This is a very smooth and creamy chocolate mousse with a quite different texture from a classic whipped egg mousse. It makes a perfect layered dessert with Whipped Strawberry Mousse, Power Granola and fresh strawberries (see page 109).

Serves 6

Special equipment
Probe thermometer

Ingredients
For the custard (makes 100ml)
1 egg yolk
10g caster sugar
50ml whipping cream
50ml whole milk
For the mousse
140g good quality dark chocolate (60% cocoa solids), broken into pieces
180ml whipping cream
To serve
White Chocolate 'Soil' (see p90)

First, make the custard. Whisk the egg yolk with the sugar in a bowl, a couple of hours in advance if possible. Heat the cream and milk in a heavy-based saucepan until simmering. Gradually whisk the hot cream and milk into the egg yolk mixture. Pour the mixture back into the saucepan and cook over a gentle heat, stirring constantly with a wooden spoon, until the mixture reaches 82–84°C, at which point it should coat the back of the spoon (be careful not to overheat the mixture, or it will scramble). Strain the custard through a fine sieve into a large clean bowl. Place the bowl in a sink of iced water to cool the mixture, stirring regularly until the temperature drops to 60°C, then cover the surface with clingfilm.

For the mousse, melt the chocolate in a bowl over a bain-marie and set aside. Reheat the custard to 60°C, if needed, over the bain-marie, then pour it on to the melted chocolate incorporating it with a rubber spatula until the mixture is smooth and glossy.

The final temperature of the chocolate custard should be 45–50°C. Whip the cream to soft peaks. Add a quarter of the whipped cream to the chocolate custard to stabilise the emulsion, beat to combine, and fold in the remaining whipped cream. Spoon or pipe the chocolate mousse into small cups or ramekins and serve immediately, sprinkled with White Chocolate 'Soil'.

DESSERTS, SAUCES, DRINKS & ICE CREAMS

107

A layered dessert made with: Crème Anglaise Chocolate Mousse (see p106), Power Granola (p186), Whipped Strawberry Mousse (p101), and strawberries as a base and garnish, with a shard of edible transfer paper to serve.

CHOCOLATE CHARLOTTE WITH RASPBERRY MOUSSE

A great dinner party dessert, this can be made a day or two in advance and served straight from the fridge. Serve it sliced, with cream or custard, and a drizzle of fruit coulis if you like.

Serves 6–8

Special equipment
2lb bread loaf tin

Ingredients
½ quantity Cocoa Sponge Fingers (i.e. 20, see p112) or 20 ladyfingers
150ml coffee, Earl Grey tea or marsala wine
500g Whipped Strawberry Mousse (see p101) made with raspberries instead of strawberries
Fruit coulis, to serve (optional)

Line the loaf tin with clingfilm. Dip the cocoa sponge fingers or ladyfingers briefly in the coffee, tea or wine to moisten them and place them inside the tin, completely covering the bottom and the sides of the tin. Chill while you make the mousse according to the method on page 101.

Spoon the mousse into the mould, cover and chill for at least 3 hours before serving. Carefully invert the charlotte on to a serving dish, and serve it in slices with a fruit coulis (if desired).

CRÈME ANGLAISE CHOCAMOUSSU

This chocolate mousse and sponge layered dessert is inspired by the classic tiramisu.

Serves 8–10

Special equipment
Rectangular 8cm-deep serving
dish or glass bowl
Disposable piping bag with 1cm
round nozzle

Ingredients
2 quantities of Crème Anglaise
Chocolate Mousse (see p106)
1 small cup (125ml) strong coffee
30ml Grand Marnier
300ml whipped cream and cocoa
powder, to finish

For the cocoa sponge fingers
(makes 30–40 fingers)
65g cornflour
30g strong white flour
30g unsweetened cocoa powder,
plus extra for dusting
6 medium eggs, separated
110g caster sugar
Icing sugar, for sprinkling
(optional)

First, make the sponge fingers. Preheat the oven to 180°C/gas mark 4 and line two large baking sheets with greaseproof paper. Sift the cornflour into a bowl with the flour and cocoa. Set to one side. Place the egg whites in a spotlessly clean bowl and whisk with an electric hand whisk set on medium speed until they are light and foamy, then add the caster sugar a little at a time, until it is fully incorporated and the mixture forms soft peaks. Using a rubber spatula or metal spoon, gently fold the egg yolks into the egg white mixture, followed by the sifted dry ingredients. Spoon the mixture into the piping bag fitted with the 1cm nozzle. Pipe the mixture into 8–10cm-long, 1cm-wide 'fingers' on the lined baking sheets, 2.5cm apart. To give them an attractive pearly crust, lightly dust them with sifted icing sugar just before baking. Bake for 14–15 minutes, until risen and cooked through. Transfer the fingers, still on the paper, to a wire rack to cool. They keep well for a day or two in an airtight container, or can be wrapped and frozen.

Make the Crème Anglaise Chocolate Mousse according to the method on page 106. Pour the coffee and liqueur into a shallow dish and moisten the sponge fingers lightly by briefly immersing them one at a time in the liquid. Place half of the sponge fingers on the bottom of the serving dish, spread a layer of half the mousse on top, then cover with the remaining soaked sponge fingers, followed by the remaining mousse. Top with whipped cream and dust liberally with sifted cocoa powder. Chill for a couple of hours before serving.

SPRING WATER GANACHE

One of the Ten Commandments when working with chocolate is 'thou shalt not mix water and chocolate', so I was surprised when some years ago I came across Fabrice Gillotte, a French chocolatier who was making truffles with spring water. Everyone said they were sublime. These days Damian Allsop has made water ganaches famous in the UK. This recipe makes a decadent dessert, but it makes great truffles too; just use a little less liquid. Be adventurous and try substituting the liquid for a light fragrant tea, such as Earl Grey or green tea. You can use Champagne, though I think it's a bit of a waste. Prosecco's just as good. This is a treat for vegans, who often miss out on rich creamy puddings.

Serves 6

Ingredients

85g Grenada Chocolate Co. chocolate (61% cocoa solids)

85g Grenada Chocolate Co. chocolate (70% cocoa solids)

170ml boiling water, or your chosen hot liquid

Crème fraîche or pouring cream, to serve (optional)

Break the chocolate into squares and place it in a heatproof bowl or jug, then cover with the boiling water or hot liquid (heated to at least 60°C). Leave it to stand for 5 minutes, then blend with a stick blender until the chocolate has completely melted. The mixture will look very thin, but will set once cool. Pour the mixture into six espresso cups or shot glasses and chill for a couple of hours, then serve immediately (it doesn't keep well). Serve with crème fraîche, if desired.

DONNA TELLA DA KIDS

This is a delicious chocolate hazelnut spread, much too good for the kids. Ultimately, it's a very posh Nutella, and you will want to keep it for yourself. If you are feeling very generous, make it in larger quantities – it makes a perfect gift.

Makes 3 x 250g jars

Special equipment
Probe thermometer

Ingredients
½ quantity Gianduja Praline
(see p52)
40g powdered milk
1 quantity Hazelnut Praline Paste
(see p46)
20g unsweetened cocoa powder
50g hazelnut butter, or 50g extra
Hazelnut Praline Paste
20g room temperature clarified
butter or ghee

Make the Gianduja Praline and place it in a large bowl over a bain-marie, heating it until it reaches 45°C. In another bowl mix together the powdered milk, Hazelnut Praline Paste, cocoa powder, hazelnut butter and clarified butter. Add these dry ingredients to the warm Gianduja Praline, mixing thoroughly until the mixture is smooth and making sure it doesn't get hotter than 30°C (or blend the ingredients together in a Thermomix, if you have one). Temper the mixture (see page 226), then pour it into sterilised jars, seal and store in a cool, dry place (not the fridge) for up to 1 month.

TWO CHOCOLATE SAUCES

Both these sauces are rich and silky, but the arguably less sophisticated water-based sauce does have the advantage of being both vegan and low in sugar. Use them to decorate a serving plate or simply pour them over ice cream or a dessert. They keep well in the fridge for a day or two, but I suggest making them freshly, especially the water one as it's very simple and quick.

Makes 400ml

Ingredients
170g Grenada Chocolate Co. chocolate
140ml milk or soya milk
35g liquid glucose

Grenada dark chocolate sauce

Put the chopped chocolate into a heatproof glass bowl. Place the milk and glucose in a heavy-based saucepan over a low heat and bring to the boil. Pour a third of the hot milk into the centre of the chopped chocolate and stir with a rubber spatula until the chocolate forms a glossy emulsion with the milk. Gradually add the rest of the milk, stirring constantly (use a stick blender if the mixture starts to separate).

Makes 200ml

Ingredients
100ml water
100g Grenada Chocolate Co. chocolate

Water-based chocolate sauce

Bring the water to the boil in a small saucepan, add the chocolate, and whisk until it thickens. Serve immediately. This sauce does not keep very well, though can be made into Hot Chocolate a l'Ancienne (see p126) if you have lots left over.

ROCOCO PRALINE CREAM

This rich dessert is a fail-safe crowd pleaser at our chocolate summer school. Serve it unadulterated in individual glasses, layer it with whipped cream, lemon cream or strawberry mousse, or pipe the chilled cream into pre-baked pastry shells. It is best made a day ahead.

Serves 12

Ingredients

50g Grenada dark couverture chocolate (71% cocoa solids), broken into pieces

175g Gianduja praline (see p52) or ready-made Gianduja 'Noisette' (see p249 for stockists), broken into pieces

10g liquid glucose or honey

3 gelatine leaves

200ml milk

350ml whipping cream

Melt both chocolates in a bowl over a bain-marie. Stir in the liquid glucose or honey, remove the bowl from the heat, and set aside.

Soften the gelatine leaves in a small bowl filled with iced water for 15 minutes. Bring the milk to the boil in a heavy-based saucepan. Remove from heat, squeeze the excess water from the gelatine leaves and add them to the hot milk, then blitz with a stick blender to encourage the gelatine to dissolve. Slowly pour the hot milk on to the melted chocolate, incorporating it with a rubber spatula until the mixture is smooth and glossy. Stir in the cream and blend with a stick blender for a few seconds, then pour it into small glasses or serving bowls. Chill overnight before serving it unadulterated, or turning it into a layered dessert.

CASSATA SERRILLI

This is a modern adaptation of the famous Sicilian cake, not the Neapolitan ice cream you might be familiar with. My very good friend Christina's family have been making this cake at Christmas time and for other celebrations for generations, with ewe's milk ricotta given to them by shepherds in return for the use of their land for grazing. Zia Giuseppina, Cristina's aunt, would mutter 'quell'odore di pecora!' and douse the strong-smelling cheese with gin after it had been strained.

Serves 15–25

Special equipment
24cm round springform cake tin

Ingredients
1½ quantities of Pistachio Marzipan (see p58)

500g good quality ricotta from an Italian deli, or 2 x 250g tubs of Ricotta Biologica

260g caster sugar

150g glacé fruit (a mixture of any of the following: lemon, orange, cedro, melon, cherry, apricot, mango) or best quality mixed candied fruit, chopped into small pieces

85g Grenada Chocolate Co. chocolate (82% cocoa solids), chopped into small pieces

2 tbsp gin

280g homemade sponge or a shop-bought Madeira cake, crusts removed, then cut into thin slices

Base-line the cake tin with greaseproof paper. Most ricotta bought in tubs is too wet, so if you have bought tub ricotta, remove it from the tub, wrap it in muslin and suspend it over a bowl to catch all the excess liquid. Leave it in a cool place to drain overnight.

Remove a 200g piece of marzipan from the 700g and set it aside. Roll out the remaining 500g of marzipan between two large pieces of clingfilm (at least 40 x 40cm) to a 30cm round, about 5mm thick. Lift the circle carefully with the edges of the clingfilm and lay it in the tin, pressing it into the bottom and sides. Remove the top layer of clingfilm.

To make the filling, mix the drained ricotta, sugar, fruit and chocolate in a bowl with 1 tbsp of gin. Spoon the mixture into the tin, then cover the filling with slices of sponge. Sprinkle with the remaining gin, and gently ease the edges of the marzipan over the sponge. Roll out the remaining 200g of marzipan to make a 24cm disc and use this to cover the sponge, sealing the edges with the handle of a teaspoon. Cover the cake with clingfilm and store it in the fridge for 2 days.

When you are ready to serve, remove the clingfilm and invert the cassata on to a serving platter, release it from the tin and peel off the rest of the clingfilm. Decorate with almonds and cherries if desired.

The cake is so rich, really the tiniest piece is all that is needed with a cup of strong espresso.

APPLE & WHITE CHOCOLATE PUDDING

I adore fruit puddings and crumbles. They are a perfect end to Sunday lunch, and the ultimate comfort food, especially when laced with white chocolate (my daughter Millie's favourite kind of chocolate when she was a child). Don't bother peeling the apples; it is pretty tedious and you are removing the most nutritious bit of the apple. You can use rhubarb, plums, apricots or any other stone or orchard fruit in place of the apples.

Serves 8

Special equipment

20 x 30 x 6cm heatproof
baking dish

Ingredients

4 dessert apples (such as Cox or
Braeburn), washed – keep the skin
on if you wish – cored and thinly
sliced (1kg prepared weight)

2 small Bramley apples, peeled,
cored and thinly sliced

350g good quality white chocolate,
broken into pieces

100g softened unsalted butter,
diced, plus extra for greasing

4 medium eggs, beaten

1 tsp vanilla extract

100g self-raising flour

100g ground almonds

A large pinch of salt

Icing sugar, for dusting (optional)

Preheat the oven to 170°C/gas mark 3. Grease the baking dish with a little butter, then cover the base with the sliced apples.

Melt 200g of the chocolate in a bowl over a bain-marie. Chop the rest of the chocolate into pea-sized pieces. Put the melted chocolate into a large mixing bowl and whisk in the butter, bit by bit, to make a light ganache. Slowly add the beaten eggs, a spoonful at a time, and continue to whisk until you have a smooth creamy mixture. Stir in the vanilla, then gently fold in the flour and ground almonds, and the rest of the chocolate and the salt. Spread the mixture on to the apples and bake for 45 minutes until golden brown on top, covering it loosely with foil if the top starts to brown too quickly. Remove from the oven and leave to rest for 5–10 minutes. Dust with icing sugar, if using, and serve warm with crème fraîche, double cream or custard.

TWO HOT CHOCOLATES

I couldn't help but include two hot chocolates here, both Rococo favourites. The Simple Hot Chocolate is a gloriously rich – yet deceptively easy to make – treat, a million miles away from the watered-down cocoa I was given at school. Hot Chocolate à l'Ancienne is a little fancier and refined: the recipe is attributed to Rosa Cannabich, a pupil of Mozart. Mozart himself was reputed to have tasted the chocolate at Mannheim in 1778. It is wonderfully unctuous, almost a meal in itself.

Serves 2 (teacup-sized servings)

Ingredients
50g good quality dark chocolate (65–70% cocoa solids), broken into small pieces

30ml whipping cream

200ml whole milk

Simple Hot Chocolate

Place the chocolate in a heatproof glass bowl. Heat the cream and milk in a small heavy-based saucepan until almost boiling, then pour it over the chocolate and leave it to melt the chocolate for a few minutes before blending it to a smooth liquid with a stick blender.

Serves 4

Ingredients
160g good quality dark chocolate (61% cocoa solids), broken into pieces, plus a little extra for grating

A small pinch of salt

50ml water

500ml milk

1 tbsp caster sugar

2 tbsp dark rum

50ml espresso coffee, or instant espresso made with 1 tsp powder and 50ml water

For the whipped cream topping
50ml crème fraîche or double cream

2 tbsp milk

1½ tsp caster sugar

Hot Chocolate à l'Ancienne

First make the whipped cream topping. Chill the bowl in which you are going to whip the cream, then add the crème fraîche or double cream, milk and sugar. Beat with an electric hand whisk until stiff, but do not overbeat or it will turn into butter. Chill until you are ready to serve the hot chocolate.

Place the chocolate in a heavy-based saucepan with the salt and water. Melt the chocolate mixture over a low heat, stirring constantly and taking great care that it does not burn. When the chocolate is smooth and shiny, stir in the milk and the sugar. Bring to a boil and simmer for 5 minutes. Be very careful because the chocolate bubbles up and thickens rapidly. Stir in the rum and coffee and boil for 2 minutes. Beat the mixture with a whisk to lighten it. When ready to serve, pour the hot chocolate into 4 serving cups, add a spoonful of the whipped cream to each portion, and top with grated chocolate.

CESAR'S SALTED CARAMEL ICE CREAM

Cesar is my nephew. He loves cooking and has had an obsession with ice cream since he spent a summer making it in New York with his other aunt, Nadia, founder of Lily Lolly's Ice Kitchen. Cesar is now developing a range of ice creams for Rococo.

Makes 1.5 litres

Special equipment

Probe thermometer

Ingredients

275g caster sugar

600ml double cream

600ml semi-skimmed milk

7 medium egg yolks

¾ tsp Maldon sea salt flakes

Flaked chocolate, to garnish

Place a clean and grease-free wide heavy-based deep saucepan over a medium heat. Once hot, put 80g of the sugar in the pan. Heat the sugar, shaking the pan regularly and stir the mixture with a wooden spoon once the sugar has melted. Add another 80g of sugar to the pan and let it melt into the first batch of melted sugar, then finally add another 80g. Once all the sugar is in the pan and caramelising, the temperature will rise quite quickly and the colour will darken to a golden caramel colour. Be careful not to over caramelise the sugar, or you will end up with a bitter flavour.

Remove the caramel from the heat and add the double cream. Be extremely careful because the mixture will splutter and spit. Bring the caramel mixture slowly back to the boil, stirring constantly to dissolve the hardened caramel, then add the milk. Whisk the caramel mixture until nearly boiling, then remove from the heat.

In a separate bowl beat the egg yolks with the remaining 35g of sugar until a pale, smooth and mousse-like sabayon. Gradually pour the hot caramel mixture on to the sabayon, whisk well, and pour into a pan and heat until 85°C. It must reach this temperature to heat treat the egg yolks. Then pass through a sieve into a clean bowl and leave it to cool on ice, then chill in the fridge overnight. Stir the salt into the chilled mixture until it has dissolved and transfer it to an ice-cream machine. Churn according to the manufacturer's instructions. Transfer the ice cream to the freezer for at least 2 hours, to allow the mix to harden before serving.

VANILLA & CHOCOLATE TRUFFLE ICE CREAM

A delicious vanilla ice cream with soft chocolate ganache swirled in at the end.

Makes 1 litre

Special equipment
Probe thermometer

Ingredients
430ml double cream
430ml semi-skimmed milk
5 medium egg yolks
190g caster sugar
1 tbsp vanilla bean paste, or the seeds from 2 large vanilla pods
½ quantity Classic Truffle ganache (see p26)

For the ice cream, bring the cream and milk to the boil in a heavy-based saucepan. Meanwhile, in a mixing bowl beat the egg yolks with the sugar until pale, smooth and mousse-like. Gradually pour the hot cream and milk mixture on to the egg yolk and sugar mixture and whisk well, then pour it back into a clean pan and cook over a low heat, stirring all the time with a wooden spoon, until it reaches 85°C and lightly coats the back of a wooden spoon. Pour the mixture through a sieve into a clean bowl, stir in the vanilla bean paste and leave it to cool on ice, then chill overnight.

The next day, transfer the vanilla custard mixture to an ice-cream machine and churn according to the manufacturer's instructions. Shortly before the ice cream has stiffened and is almost ready, make the chocolate ganache according to the method on page 26.

Spoon half the ice cream mixture into a plastic box and spoon over half of the still slightly warm chocolate ganache in lines. Cover with the remaining ice cream and the remaining ganache, then zig-zag the handle of a wooden spoon through the mixture to ripple it. Transfer the ice cream to the freezer for at least 2 hours. Remove it from the freezer and let it soften for 10–15 minutes before serving.

PRALINE-FILLED HEN'S EGGS

These filled hen's eggs are a perfect way of tricking small children, who will be thrilled by the chocolate filling, and we have been selling them for decades at Easter – they are a Rococo classic. Serve them for breakfast, high tea or as a dessert at the end of a dinner party. If you want to get really clever, you can fill quail's eggs. It takes more skill, as they are so small and the shells are quite soft, but it's well worth the extra effort. Wash the quail's eggs before you start, as they are not always very clean.

Makes 6 large filled eggs

Special equipment
Spring-loaded egg topper
Paring knife
Disposable piping bag fitted with a 5mm round nozzle (optional)

Ingredients
6 large, fresh organic eggs
½ quantity Gianduja Praline (see p48)
1 quantity Donna Tella Da Kids (see p117)
Slices of toasted brioche, grissini breadsticks, or grilled slices of bacon for dipping

Use the special spring-loaded egg topper to delicately remove the tops from 6 large eggs, holding the bottom of each egg with a paper towel or tea towel as you pull up the plunger on the tool, and drop it 2 or 3 times to cut the shell. If you need to, insert a small paring knife into the incision made by the egg-top cutter, to prise the top off (this takes a little practice, but delve into YouTube and you'll find helpful clips).

Pour the egg whites and yolks into a bowl, ready to use in another recipe. Peel the membrane away from the shell and sterilise the empty shells; place them in a large saucepan of cold water, bring to the boil, then turn off the heat and leave them in the hot water for 20 minutes. Stand them open-side down on a wire rack covered in a layer of kitchen paper to cool and dry for a few hours, or place the wire rack on a baking tray in the oven at its lowest setting for 10 minutes.

Place each egg shell open-top up in the egg box, and pipe in the Gianduja Praline (see page 52) using a piping bag fitted with a 5mm round nozzle or homemade paper piping bag (see page 74). Chill for up to an hour – you don't want the praline to set completely – and serve in egg cups with toasted brioche or grissini for dipping, or go 'extreme' and serve it with freshly grilled maple cured smoked bacon, dipped into tempered chocolate and left to set before serving (see page 134).

Note: if the eggs are stored in the fridge, put them in the microwave for 30 second bursts, until the filling has reached the desired consistency.

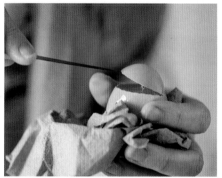

135

TARTS & PAS— TRIES

CHOCOLATE CRUNCH ECLAIRS

These éclairs are modelled on the glazed éclairs you find in patisseries and bakeries, but they are markedly different. They have a crunchy pastry layer on the top, instead of a smooth icing, and a rich, smooth chocolate crème pâtissière filling.

Makes 20 éclairs

Special equipment
Disposable piping bag with plain nozzles (12mm and 5mm)

Ingredients

For the chocolate crème pâtissière
500ml whole milk

250ml whipping cream

8 medium egg yolks

70g caster sugar

50g cornflour

340g Grenada Chocolate Co. chocolate (71% cocoa solids), chopped into small pieces

For the cocoa crunch
40g unsalted butter, softened

55g demerera sugar

45g plain flour

10g cocoa powder

For the choux pastry
140g plain flour

125ml water

125ml whole milk

110g unsalted butter

4g salt

1 tsp caster sugar

4 medium eggs, beaten, plus extra for brushing

To make the chocolate crème pâtissière, heat the milk and cream in a non-stick saucepan until boiling. Meanwhile, whisk the egg yolks with the sugar in a bowl until smooth, then whisk in the cornflour. Whisk in a little of the hot milk and cream to loosen it, then whisk in the remainder. Return the mixture to the pan, place it over a medium heat and cook, whisking continuously, until the mixture reaches boiling point. After about 1 minute it will thicken and become light and glossy. Take the pan off the heat, leave to cool slightly for 3–4 minutes, then add the chopped chocolate, and whisk, or blend with a stick blender, until you have a smooth and glossy emulsion. Pour it into a container lined with clingfilm and place more clingfilm on the surface to stop it forming a skin. Chill for at least 2 hours. When you are ready to use it, transfer the mixture to a clean bowl and whisk by hand, or using a hand-held electric hand whisk or free-standing food mixer, until smooth.

For the cocoa crunch, place the butter and sugar in a bowl and mix until creamy. Sift the flour and cocoa powder over the butter and sugar, and beat to combine. Place the dough between two sheets of greaseproof paper and roll it out into a rectangle that measures roughly 20 x 22cm (approximately 2mm thick). Place it in the freezer, keeping it flat until firm; about 30 minutes. Remove the top sheet of greaseproof paper and cut the cocoa crunch mixture into twenty 11 x 2cm rectangles. Keep in the fridge until needed.

For the choux pastry, sift the flour into a bowl and set aside. Put the water, milk, butter, salt and sugar in a saucepan and place over a low heat until the butter has melted. Then increase the heat to high and rapidly bring the mixture to the boil. Take the pan off the heat, tip in the flour, and beat vigorously with a wooden spoon until the mixture is smooth. Place the pan back over a medium heat and cook the mixture for 3 minutes, stirring continuously to dry it out a little. Tip the paste into the bowl of a free-standing food mixer, fitted with the paddle attachment, mix the paste and leave to cool for a few minutes. Then with the machine on low speed, very gradually add enough of the beaten egg to form a smooth and glossy paste that drops reluctantly from a spoon. You might not need to add it all.

Line 2 large baking sheets with non-stick baking paper or silicone mats. Spoon the paste into a piping bag fitted with the 12mm plain nozzle and pipe out buns measuring about 10cm long and 3cm across, spaced at least 5cm apart. Place a piece of cocoa crunch on top of each éclair. Bake in an oven at 180°C/gas mark 4 for 25 minutes and then turn the oven temperature down (do not open the oven, or the éclairs will collapse) to 150°C/gas mark 2 and bake for a further 15 minutes until they are crisp, dry and golden brown. Cool on a wire rack and store in an airtight container until needed (they also freeze well).

To serve, split the éclairs in half horizontally. Either spoon the chocolate crème pâtissière into a piping bag fitted with the 5mm nozzle or use a teaspoon. Pipe or spoon the chocolate crème pâtissière along the bottom half of each éclair. Replace the top half of the éclairs and serve immediately.

CHOC-EN-BOUCHE

We created this as a chocolate tribute to the classic French 'croquembouche'. There is no denying that it is complex to make, but it is well worth the effort and it makes a great showpiece for a special event. It can be made over 2 days if necessary: the choux buns and pastry cream on day one and the tempered chocolate and cone on day two.

Serves 10–12

Special equipment
Disposable piping bag with plain nozzles (5mm for filling the buns, and 12mm for piping the choux)
Polystyrene cone 27cm high, 12cm wide at the base (see p249 for stockists)
Cocoa butter transfer sheets or sheets of acetate (see p249 for stockists)

Ingredients
1 quantity Chocolate Crème Pâtissière (see p138)
1 quantity Choux Pastry (see p138), makes 70–80 balls
1kg good quality dark chocolate, tempered (see p226–228), for the base and for dipping
Silver almond dragées

Make the chocolate crème pâtissière, then make the choux paste.

Bake the choux buns

Spoon the choux paste into a disposable piping bag fitted with the 12mm plain nozzle and pipe out round buns measuring about 3cm across, spaced at least 5cm apart, on to silicone mats or greased baking sheets. Lightly brush the buns with a little beaten egg and bake in batches at 150°C/gas mark 2 for 25–30 minutes. Don't be tempted to open the oven door, or the buns might collapse. They should be golden and cooked through. Remove from the oven and leave to cool on a wire rack. Store in an airtight container until needed (they also freeze well).

Fill the choux buns

Make a hole in the flat side of each choux bun with the tip of the 5mm piping nozzle. Whisk the chilled crème pâtissière in the bowl of a free-standing food mixer until smooth, spoon it into a piping bag with the 5mm nozzle and fill each bun with cream. Wipe off any excess cream on the outside of the buns, and transfer them to the fridge.

Make the chocolate base

Pour 200g of the tempered chocolate on to an acetate sheet or cocoa butter transfer sheet and spread it into a 22cm diameter circle with a stepped palette knife. When the chocolate starts to solidify, cut a neat circle 20cm in diameter with a sharp knife, using a plate or saucepan lid as a guide. Once you have removed the template, slide the chocolate

round on to a baking tray. Place a piece of greaseproof paper or silicone sheet on top of the chocolate, and place another baking tray on top (this helps prevent the disc curling up at the edges). Invert both trays, holding them together, so that the bottom tray is facing up, and leave in a cool place for an hour or two for the chocolate to set and crystallise.

Dip the choux buns

Dip the rounded side of each filled bun into tempered chocolate, lifting the bun up and down to remove excess chocolate – you want to cover three-quarters of the bun's surface. Place them chocolate side down on another cocoa butter transfer sheet, sitting on top of a baking sheet. When you have dipped all the buns, and placed them all on the transfer sheet, chill them for 15 minutes so that the chocolate sets.

Assemble the choc-en-bouche

Wrap the outside of the polystyrene cone well with clingfilm, making sure all surfaces are covered, including the base. Stand it on a large square of silicone paper, which will make it easier to turn around when you are building the cone. Brush a small area at the base of the cone with tempered chocolate (only brush a small area at a time otherwise it will set). Starting with slightly larger buns, if they are not all uniform size, dip one side of the bun in the tempered chocolate and then on to the brushed area of the cone. Continue with more large buns, sticking them to each other and the cone as you go, until you have made a full circle of buns around the base, like a collar. Using the same technique, move on to the next layer up the cone. This time dip two sides of the buns, one to stick to the previously placed layer of buns, the other to stick to the bun by its side. Continue dipping and placing the buns, letting the chocolate set for a few minutes after assembling each layer, and selecting the best size of bun to fit the gap. Use the smallest buns to finish the cone and stick one on the top. You will need to reheat your chocolate to keep it tempered because it will cool down quite quickly. When the whole cone is covered, leave it to set for 15 minutes in the fridge.

Remove the top tray from the chocolate base, followed by the acetate or transfer sheet, and remove the trimmings. Delicately turn your masterpiece upside down and, with a little help, gently remove the cone and the clingfilm. You don't have to do this, however, as the polystyrene cone probably won't be visible. Use some of the tempered chocolate to stick the cone of choux buns to the base and to secure the silver almond dragées in place. It is best served immediately, but will keep for a short time if chilled. Serve the choc-en-bouche at the table and let your guests demolish all your hard work (once they have praised you first, of course). Serve with crème anglaise or vanilla ice cream.

WHITE CHOCOLATE & LIME TART

Robert Mantho, an American friend often mistaken for Robert de Niro, makes a mean key lime pie with tiny limes from Miami. This is my homage to the American classic. You can make a simpler crushed biscuit base, which my daughter Millie prefers, by mixing 300g of crushed digestive biscuits with 80g of melted butter and pressing the mixture into the base of the tin. The filling is a silky curd made with white chocolate; a perfect contrast to the sharp limes.

Serves 8–10

Special equipment

2.5cm deep x 24cm loose-
bottomed flan tin

Disposable piping bag fitted with
round nozzle (optional)

Ingredients

For the pastry

145g plain flour, plus extra for
dusting

15g Valrhona cocoa powder

45g icing sugar, plus extra for
dusting

A pinch of salt

95g chilled unsalted butter, diced,
plus extra for greasing

1 medium egg yolk

1 tsp iced water (optional)

For the curd filling

Finely grated zest of 1 unwaxed
lemon and 2 limes

250ml fresh lemon and lime juice
(approximately 3 lemons and
4 limes)

80g caster sugar

5 medium eggs, beaten

200g good quality white chocolate

Start by making the pastry. Sift the flour, cocoa powder and icing sugar into a bowl and add the salt. Transfer to a food processor, add the butter and blitz with a metal blade until the mixture resembles fine breadcrumbs. Add the egg yolk and pulse gently until you have a lump of smooth, soft dough. If it doesn't quite come together, add the ice-cold water. Wrap the dough in clingfilm and chill for 1–2 hours to firm up.

Preheat the oven to 190°C/gas mark 5 and generously grease the base and sides of the flan tin. Roll out the pastry on a lightly floured surface, and ease it gently into the tin, pressing it into and up the sides, trimming off any excess. Don't worry if the pastry breaks; roll out the excess pastry and use it to patch up any gaps or tears. Prick the pastry all over with a fork and chill for 20 minutes, then line it with a large sheet of greaseproof paper and cover the base with a layer of baking beans. Blind bake the pastry for 15 minutes, remove the paper and beans, and return the pastry to the oven for a further 7–8 minutes or until cooked through. Set aside to cool before filling.

Now make the curd filling. Place the lemon and half the lime zest, the juices and the sugar in a heatproof bowl, then place the bowl over a bain-marie. Stir occasionally with a wooden spoon until the sugar has dissolved. Add the beaten eggs to the bowl and cook over a low heat, whisking continuously with an electric hand whisk on medium speed for 15–20 minutes, until the mixture is thick and moussey and reaches 70°C – but be careful not to get the mixture too hot, or you will get scrambled eggs. Remove the bowl from the heat. Melt the white chocolate in a separate bowl over the bain-marie, and pour it into the lemon curd. Fold it in gently with a rubber spatula to emulsify the two mixtures. Cover and chill for at least 6 hours. Once cool, spoon or pipe the filling on to the pastry base and spread out evenly. Sprinkle over the zest of the remaining lime and serve, cut into wedges.

APRICOT & LAVENDER TART

A lovely summery tart made with fresh apricots and lavender, and a chocolate almond filling. The richness of the chocolate is balanced out by the acidity of the fruit. You can make the lavender sugar in advance, infusing the sugar with the lavender heads in a sealed container for a month or two, removing the lavender before using the sugar.

Serves 6–8

Special equipment

3–4cm deep x 23cm loose-bottomed flan tin

Ingredients

For the pastry

160g plain flour, plus extra for dusting

20g ground almonds

80g softened unsalted butter, diced

1 medium egg yolk

1 tsp iced water

A pinch of salt

60g icing sugar

For the lavender-sugar apricots

6 fresh lavender heads

2 tbsp soft brown sugar

6 fresh apricots, halved and stoned

1 tbsp unsalted butter, melted

For the frangipane filling

150g Grenada Chocolate Co. chocolate (71% cocoa solids), broken into pieces

75g icing sugar

10g cornflour

225g ground almonds

160ml milk

2 large eggs, beaten

To make the pastry, mix 50g of the flour and the ground almonds in a large bowl with the butter, egg yolk, water, salt and sugar. Using your hands, gradually work in the rest of the flour and continue to knead, creating a soft smooth dough. Wrap the dough in clingfilm and chill for an hour or two to firm up. While the dough is chilling, make the lavender sugar by crushing the flower heads with the sugar in a pestle and mortar. Place the apricot halves cut-side up on a baking tray lined with foil and brush them with melted butter. Sprinkle each apricot with the lavender sugar and grill for 2–3 minutes until sizzling and lightly browned. Set aside to cool.

Bring the pastry back to room temperature. Roll it out thinly on a lightly floured surface, then roll it up on to the rolling pin and unroll it over the flan tin, using your thumbs to coax it into the inner edges. Prick the base with a fork and chill for 20 minutes.

Place a baking tray in the oven and preheat it to 200°C/gas mark 6. Line the pastry with baking parchment or greaseproof paper, and cover the base with a layer of baking beans. Place on the baking tray and bake for 15 minutes, until the edges of the pastry are golden brown. Remove the paper and beans, and return it to the oven for 5–6 minutes until the base of the pastry case is lightly golden. Remove and leave to cool. Reduce the oven temperature to 150°C/gas mark 2. Melt the chocolate and set aside. Sift the icing sugar and cornflour into a bowl and stir in the ground almonds. Bring the milk to the boil and pour it into the almond mixture, beating it to make a batter, then whisk in the eggs. Stir a quarter of the batter, a spoon at a time, into the melted chocolate, then pour the chocolatey mixture back into the remaining batter. Mix thoroughly, spoon the batter into the pastry case and spread it out evenly. Arrange the apricots cut-side up on top and bake the tart for 45–50 minutes. The filling should be firm and a skewer pushed into the centre should come away with a few sticky crumbs on it. Remove from the oven and leave to cool in the tin.

CAKES, BAKES & BIS—CUITS

DORLI PERCIVAL'S VIENNESE TORTE

I met Dorli many times over the years at her family's parties. She was always most charming and insisted that I make this celebration cake with her, the recipe for which has been in her family for at least five generations, so that I could put it into my book. Sadly we never got around to it before she died, but with great pleasure her daughter Kate, guardian of the recipe and the family's chief cake maker, and I recently made the cake together. It is far better to my mind than the famous Viennese Sacher. Dorli would not have approved of my chocolate glaze with gelatin, not the Viennese tradition!

Serves 15–20

Special equipment
2 x 20cm springform cake tins

Ingredients
For the cake
175g whole almonds with their skins on

50g plain flour

225g Grenada Chocolate Co. chocolate (70% cocoa solids)

8 large eggs, separated

225g caster sugar

225g softened unsalted butter, diced

25g white chocolate, broken into small pieces, to decorate

For the apricot glaze
200g good quality apricot jam

Juice of 1 lemon

For the chocolate glaze
3 gelatine leaves

135g granulated sugar

50ml water

37g unsweetened cocoa powder

45ml whipping cream

50g good quality dark chocolate (70% cocoa solids), broken in pieces

Preheat the oven to 160°C/gas mark 3. Grease the tins, and line the base and sides of with greaseproof paper.

Blitz the almonds in a food processor until they are roughly ground (not powdery), then mix them in a bowl with flour. Melt the chocolate in a bowl over a bain-marie.

Cream the egg yolks with the sugar in the bowl of an electric mixer until pale and fluffy, then add the butter and continue to mix until combined. Place the egg whites in a spotlessly clean bowl and beat with a clean electric hand whisk with a pinch of salt until they form stiff peaks.

Mix the melted chocolate into the egg yolk mixture, one spoon at a time, then gradually and gently fold in the egg whites with a large metal spoon, alternating with a spoon of the almond and flour mixture.

Divide the cake mixture evenly between the two prepared tins and smooth the tops. Bake for 35–45 minutes, or until a skewer inserted into the centre of the cakes comes out with just a few moist crumbs stuck to it. Turn the cakes out on to a wire rack and leave to cool. Blitz the apricot jam in a blender with the lemon juice. If it's too thick, gently warm it through and pass it through a sieve. Remove the paper from the cakes, and paint the apricot glaze over both, starting at the top and working out and down over the sides. Leave in a cool place.

Meanwhile, make the chocolate glaze. Soften the gelatine leaves in a small bowl filled with iced water for 5 minutes. In a saucepan, combine the sugar, water, cocoa powder and whipping cream. Bring to the boil and simmer for 1 minute. Take the pan off the heat, squeeze the excess water from the gelatine and add it to the hot sauce with the chocolate

pieces. Blitz with a stick blender, or stir vigorously, until the chocolate and gelatine have melted. Set aside to cool.

Stack the two apricot-glazed cakes on a wire rack over a baking tray (to catch any drips). Pour the chocolate glaze slowly on to the middle of the cake and work outwards and down the sides using a palette knife or rubber spatula. Try not to overwork the glaze; you want a really shiny cake. Leave to set at room temperature.

To decorate the cake, melt 20g of the white chocolate in a small bowl over a mug of boiling water (white chocolate melts very quickly). Once it has melted add the remaining 5g of chocolate and stir until melted – this is a basic way of tempering, called the 'seeding' method (see page 228). Put half the melted chocolate into a small paper cone and cut the tip so you have a very small opening, and pipe letters or shapes on the top of the cake. Refill the paper cone with the remaining chocolate if necessary.

Serve sliced, with very cold whipped cream. This keeps for a few days in the fridge.

REINE DE SABA

This gluten-free chocolate and almond cake is simple yet decadent, and very quick to make.

Serves 8–10

Special equipment

24cm round springform cake tin

Ingredients

1 tbsp plain flour, for dusting

180g good quality dark chocolate, broken into pieces

250g softened unsalted butter, plus extra for greasing

175g soft brown sugar

100g ground almonds

6 medium eggs

1 tsp cider vinegar

Unsweetened cocoa powder and icing sugar, for dusting

Crème fraîche or ice cream, to serve

Lightly butter the tin and line the bottom with baking parchment, then dust with flour, shaking out any excess. Preheat the oven to 170°C/ gas mark 3.

Melt the chocolate in a bowl over a bain-marie.

In a large bowl, cream the butter and sugar until pale and fluffy, then add the ground almonds and mix thoroughly. Stir in the melted chocolate, then beat in the eggs, one at a time, until combined. Stir in the vinegar, which helps to stop the top cracking.

Spoon the mixture into the prepared tin, and bake for 30–35 minutes, or until it is firm to the touch but not cooked through: the cake will still be very moist inside, and a skewer inserted into the centre of the cake will not come out completely clean.

Remove the cake from the oven and leave it to cool in the tin (don't worry if it sinks in the middle), then remove and sprinkle with cocoa powder and icing sugar. Serve with crème fraîche or ice cream.

WHITE CHOCOLATE, CAMPARI, ORANGE & CHERRY CAKE

This sits happily somewhere between a cake and a pudding. Inspired by Claudia Roden's boiled orange and almond cake, it is dense and fruity, and the combination of Campari, orange and white chocolate works beautifully. You can make it without the cherries, if they are not in season, and you can make it gluten-free by replacing the self-raising flour with cornflour.

Serves 8–10

Special equipment

900g loaf tin, measuring approximately 22 x 12 x 7cm

Ingredients

1 large orange

300g good quality white chocolate

100g blanched almonds

100g skinned hazelnuts

100g self-raising flour

100g softened unsalted butter

225g caster sugar

3 large eggs

200g pitted fresh morello cherries or a 425g can of pitted cherries in light syrup, well drained

3 tbsp Campari

Juice the orange, setting aside the juice to use later, then cut the peel into 5mm-thick strips. Place the peel in a small saucepan and cover with cold water, bring to the boil and simmer for 15 minutes. Drain and repeat. Drain well, then blitz in a food processor until smooth.

Preheat the oven to 170°C/gas mark 3. Grease and line the loaf tin with non-stick baking paper.

Melt the white chocolate over a bain-marie and set to one side. Blitz the almonds and hazelnuts in a food processor until finely chopped, then add the flour and blitz a little more until very fine. Cream the butter with 100g of the caster sugar until light and fluffy. Beat in the eggs, one at a time, adding a heaped tablespoon of the nut and flour mixture with the last 2 eggs to stop the mixture from curdling. Fold in the melted chocolate followed by the remaining nut and flour mixture, the orange purée, and finally the cherries. Spoon the mixture into the prepared tin and bake for approximately 1¼ hours, covering loosely with foil after about 45 minutes if it starts to brown too quickly. A skewer inserted into the centre of the cake should come away clean.

Meanwhile, for the Campari and orange syrup, strain the orange juice through a sieve into a measuring jug and make the liquid up to 125ml with water. Pour into a small saucepan, add the remaining 125g of sugar and warm through over a low heat until the sugar has dissolved. Bring to the boil and simmer for 5 minutes. Remove from the heat, stir in the Campari and set aside. Remove the cake from the oven and slowly spoon over half of the syrup. You can store the remainder in a sealed jar for another cake. Leave for 5 minutes, to let the syrup soak in, then remove the cake from the tin and leave to cool on a wire rack.

MILK CHOCOLATE & PASSION FRUIT SHORTBREAD

This is a special celebration cake, made in the French pastry chef tradition. It requires some skill to decorate it as we have done here, but you can leave out the chocolate disc and it will be just as delicious: simply make the base, spread it with the ganache, then decorate it with raspberries or passion fruit pulp or both.

Serves 10–12

Special equipment

23cm loose-bottomed sandwich tin

Sheet of acetate (see p249 for stockists)

Disposable piping bag fitted with 12mm round nozzle

Ingredients

For the milk chocolate shortbread

3 medium egg yolks

96g caster sugar

96g softened unsalted butter, cut into small dice, plus extra for greasing

135g plain flour

5g baking powder

A large pinch of fine table salt (about 1g)

30g good quality milk chocolate, cut into pea-sized pieces

For the milk chocolate ganache

340g milk chocolate couverture (33% cocoa solids), chopped into small pieces

200ml sieved passion fruit juice (approximately 20 fruit)

30g liquid glucose

For the chocolate disc

200g good quality dark chocolate, tempered (see p226–228)

To finish

150g fresh raspberries

The pulp from 2 passion fruit

For the shortbread, beat the egg yolks and sugar together in a mixing bowl until pale and creamy. Beat in the butter, a couple of pieces at a time, until thoroughly combined. Sift the flour, baking powder and salt together, then add it to the egg yolk and sugar mixture and mix until well combined. Stir in the milk chocolate pieces. Turn the mixture out on to a lightly floured work surface and shape into a smooth ball. Place between 2 large sheets of clingfilm, flatten slightly into a disc, and chill for 20 minutes.

Meanwhile, preheat the oven to 160°C/gas mark 3. Grease the sandwich tin with butter and line the base with greaseproof paper.

Remove the shortbread dough from the fridge and roll it out between the sheets of clingfilm, into a 23cm disc. Remove the top piece of clingfilm and carefully transfer it to the prepared tin. Remove the second sheet of clingfilm and press out the dough in an even layer over the base of the tin. Prick the dough a couple of times with a fork, put it on the middle shelf of the oven and reduce the oven temperature to 150°C/gas mark 2. Bake for 25–30 minutes until pale golden brown. Remove and leave to cool in the tin on a wire rack.

For the ganache, melt the chocolate over a bain-marie. Remove the bowl from the heat and set aside. Put the passion fruit juice in a small heavy-based saucepan with the liquid glucose and heat gently until almost boiling.

Slowly pour the hot passion fruit juice on to the melted chocolate, incorporating it with a rubber spatula until the mixture is smooth and glossy. Pour the mixture into a shallow dish, cover with clingfilm and chill until almost set but still pipeable (1–2 hours).

For the chocolate disc, mark a 23cm disc on to a sheet of acetate using the base of the sandwich tin as a template. Spread the tempered chocolate on the acetate within the marked disc and leave it to set for a few minutes, then place the template on top of the chocolate and cut around it to make a disc. Remove the template and slide the chocolate on to a baking tray. Place a piece of greaseproof paper or silicone and another baking tray on top of the disc. Holding the trays together, invert them and leave to cool for an hour or two. Cut the disc into 10–12 evenly sized wedges with a small paring knife. Leave for 10–15 minutes to set.

Carefully remove the shortbread from the tin and transfer it to a flat serving plate. Spoon the ganache into the disposable piping bag and pipe in a spiral, starting from the centre, on top of the shortbread, leaving a 1cm wide strip around the edge.

Arrange the raspberries around the edge of the shortbread in pairs, leaving a 1cm-gap between each pair. Angle the chocolate wedges between the raspberries and then spoon some of the passion fruit pulp between each wedge on top of the ganache.

Serve cut into wedges.

MRS PRIZEMAN'S CHOCOLATE CLUB SANDWICHES

The history of the Prizemans and Langans is well documented. John Prizeman designed the original Langan's Brasserie for Peter Langan in 1976. John's son Mark worked, at the age of 15, as a commis chef at Odin's, which is part of Langan's Group, and made this signature cake many times, before becoming an architect. These days I work closely with him on the interior design of all our shops, and he has generously shared this special recipe. The family refer to the recipe as Mrs Prizeman's, although it came originally from Mrs Langan. For a lavish finish, serve it with chocolate sauce.

Makes 8 sandwiches

Special equipment
21 x 30 x 5cm shallow, rectangular cake or brownie tin (buttered and lined with baking paper)
8 bamboo cocktail sticks, to serve

Ingredients
For the chocolate sponge
6 large eggs
65g caster sugar
45g unsweetened cocoa powder, sifted
To finish
250ml double cream
¼ quantity Classic Truffle ganache (see p26)
75–100g fresh blueberries, halved
150g fresh raspberries, halved

For the chocolate sponge, preheat the oven to 160°C/gas mark 3.

In a table top mixer with a balloon whisk beat the eggs with the sugar until the sugar has dissolved and you have a light and fluffy mousse-like mixture. The whisk should leave a ribbon trail in the mixture when lifted, and it should have trebled or quadrupled in volume. Add the cocoa powder one heaped teaspoonful at a time, stirring gently until well combined. The mixture will deflate slightly but don't worry. Pour the cake mixture into the prepared tin and bake on the middle shelf of the oven for 20 minutes until it is firm to the touch, and a skewer inserted into the cake comes away clean. Remove the cake from the oven and remove it from the tin. Carefully release the paper from the sides of the cake while it is still warm so that the cake retains its rectangular shape as it cools. Leave to cool on a wire rack.

To assemble the sandwiches, trim the edges off the cake and cut into 6 squares with a serrated knife. Cut each square diagonally in half into triangles and then carefully slice each triangle of 'bread' horizontally in half. It is the inside faces of the cut sponge cake that resemble sliced bread.

Whip the cream to soft peaks. For each sandwich, spread the uncut side of 2 triangles of cake with 1 tablespoon of the ganache. Arrange some halved blueberries on one piece and some halved raspberries on the other. Spread a little whipped cream over the fruit. Place the blueberry-covered triangle on to a serving plate and carefully cover with the raspberry covered triangle. Top with a third slice of sponge, cut-side facing up. Spear with a cocktail stick as you would a club sandwich. Repeat the process for the remaining sandwiches.

SEA SALT MILK CHOCOLATE MADELEINES AU MIEL

Proust's classic childhood recipe. The batter is traditionally made the day before and left to rest, but I find they taste just us good if eaten on the day they are made.

Makes approximately 30 madeleines

Special equipment
2 x 12-hole madeleine tins
Disposable piping bag
(no nozzle required)

Ingredients
200g unsalted butter, plus extra
for greasing
3 medium eggs at room
temperature
100g caster sugar
50g honey
½ vanilla pod, split lengthways
and seeds scraped out
A large pinch of salt (about 1g)
200g self-raising flour, sifted, plus
extra for dusting
60ml whole milk
30g good quality milk chocolate
such as Rococo Sea Salt, chopped
into pea-sized pieces

Grease the madeleine tins with butter and dust them lightly with flour. Preheat the oven to 230°C/gas mark 8.

Melt the butter in a large saucepan over a medium-high heat and leave it to bubble for about 5 minutes until it browns to a light hazelnut colour. Pour it into a heatproof bowl to stop it cooking any further and set aside to cool slightly.

Place the eggs, sugar, honey, vanilla seeds and salt in a large bowl and whisk with an electric hand mixer (or do this in a free-standing food mixer) until the mixture is very thick, light and fluffy, and the whisk leaves a 'ribbon' trail in the mixture when lifted and moved in a figure of eight above the bowl. Sift the flour over the egg mixture and fold it in with a large metal spoon or a spatula. Carefully fold in the lukewarm melted butter, the milk and the chopped milk chocolate.

Spoon the batter into a disposable piping bag without a nozzle so that the chocolate chips can pass through. Pipe into the prepared moulds, not filling each compartment more than half full. Place the trays in the oven and cook for 5 minutes. Then, turn off the oven, don't open the oven door, and leave the cakes to cook for another 3 minutes; the residual heat will continue to cook them. When they are risen, golden and springy to the touch, remove them from the oven and set aside to cool. Remove the madeleines from the tins and store them in an airtight container for up to 3 days.

FLOURLESS CHOCOLATE CAKE WITH RASPBERRIES

This great French cake recipe was handed down to Laurent Couchaux, one of our past chocolatiers, by his grandmother. Made with cornflour and ground almonds, it is gluten-free, perfect for anyone with an intolerance to wheat. The cake is best made the day before it is eaten.

Serves 8–10

Special equipment

Deep 20cm square loose-bottomed cake tin

Ingredients

140g Grenada Chocolate Co. dark chocolate (71% cocoa solids), broken into pieces

85g unsalted butter, plus extra, melted, for greasing

85g ground almonds

20g cornflour

5 medium eggs, separated

100g caster sugar, plus extra for sprinkling

120g frozen raspberries

Preheat the oven to 180°C/gas mark 6. Brush the insides of the cake tin with melted butter and line the base with non-stick baking paper. Sprinkle the greased tin with caster sugar.

Melt the chocolate and butter together in a large bowl over a bain-marie, and set aside to cool slightly. Mix the ground almonds with the cornflour in another large bowl.

In a spotlessly clean bowl, beat the egg whites with a clean electric hand whisk until frothy. Add half the sugar and continue to beat, moving the whisk around the bowl to catch all the mixture. When the mixture is thick and forms soft peaks, add the remaining sugar and continue to beat until it forms soft, stiff and shiny peaks.

Stir the egg yolks into the melted chocolate. Do not worry if it seems too thick, it will loosen up with the egg whites. Loosen the mixture by vigorously beating in two large spoonfuls of the egg white mixture. With a large metal spoon, add the remaining egg whites to the chocolate a spoonful at a time, mixing gently to combine between each addition. Gently fold in the ground almond and cornflour mixture. Pour the light mousse-like mixture into the prepared tin, and gently arrange the raspberries on the top, pushing them in a little, but leaving the fruit showing. You must use the raspberries straight from the freezer as they will 'bleed' if they are fresh.

Bake for 30–35 minutes until just cooked; a skewer inserted should come out with just a few sticky crumbs on it. Remove the cake from the oven and leave it to cool in the tin before turning out to serve. If making a day ahead, store in the fridge.

CHOCOLATE ROULADE

I first met Paul de Bondt and his wife Cecilia in 1996 at the Eurochocolate festival in Perugia. Based in Pisa, he is one of the best chocolatiers and pastry chefs in Tuscany. We spent a weekend teaching together at a cookery school and this is one of his recipes, a classic light chocolatey Genoise sponge that makes the perfect foil to a creamy filling or ganache, and is a lovely celebration cake.

Serves 8–10

Special equipment

23 x 33cm Swiss roll tin or baking tin

Ingredients

A little melted butter, for greasing

56g plain flour

20g unsweetened cocoa powder, plus extra for dusting

3 large eggs, separated

A pinch of salt

75g caster sugar, plus extra for dusting

1 tbsp icing sugar, for dusting (optional)

For the filling

½ quantity of Whipped Strawberry Mousse (see p101), or 250g Classic Truffle ganache (see p26) with 200ml double cream, whipped to soft peaks

Make your desired filling before you start to make your roulade. You will need to start the whipped strawberry mousse the night before. Otherwise make the ganache and chill it until just thick enough to spread.

Preheat the oven to 200°C/gas mark 6. Grease the Swiss roll tin or baking tin with a little melted butter, line with greaseproof paper or parchment, and grease the paper or parchment.

Sift the flour and cocoa powder together into a large bowl. Put the egg whites in a spotlessly clean bowl with the salt and a quarter of the sugar, and beat with an electric hand whisk until thick and light. Gradually add the remaining sugar, continuing to beat the mixture until it is stiff and glossy (but not dry). Beat the egg yolks in a bowl to break them up and gradually fold them into the meringue mixture, then gently fold in the flour and cocoa with a large metal spoon or spatula until well combined, keeping in as much air as possible.

Turn the sponge mixture into the lined tin, level it out with a palette knife or spatula, and bake for 6–8 minutes, or until risen and springy to the touch. Remove the tray from the oven, fold back the edges of paper and carefully invert it on to a sheet of baking paper generously dusted with caster sugar, leaving the paper on the back. Cover with a damp tea towel and leave to cool. Once the sponge is cool, peel off the paper.

Spread the Whipped Strawberry Mousse or Classic Truffle ganache over the sponge with a palette knife, leaving a 2cm margin of sponge around all the edges. If using Classic Truffle ganache, cover it with a layer of whipped cream. Pick up one of the short ends of the paper and let the sponge slowly roll gently on to itself, encouraging it with the paper, forming a roll. Wrap the roulade in greaseproof paper and chill for an hour to firm up. Just before serving, dust with cocoa powder or icing sugar.

THE AFFINITIES CAKE

I came across a simpler version of this vegan-friendly cake in Grenada, when it was made for Mott Green, co-founder of the Grenada Chocolate Company, by Kate Bauman at Almost Paradise Cottages. My version of the 'volcanic' cake was created for the 10th anniversary of Deutsche Bank and Solomon R. Guggenheim's collaboration. It is a triumph of alchemy and is very simple to make. The iced cake improves with being kept for a day.

Serves 8–10

Special equipment
Deep 20cm round cake tin, or loose-bottomed 20cm cake tin

Ingredients
200g plain flour
75g unsweetened cocoa powder
1 tsp bicarbonate of soda
200g golden caster sugar
100g ground almonds
A small pinch of salt
1 tsp vanilla extract
1 tbsp good quality balsamic vinegar
6 tbsp olive oil, plus extra for greasing
400ml prune juice
fresh pink rose petals, to decorate
For the icing
170g good quality dark chocolate
150ml whipping cream

Preheat the oven to 150°C/gas mark 2. Grease the insides of the cake tin with olive oil and line the bottom of the tin with greaseproof paper. If you are using a loose-bottomed tin, double-line it with greaseproof paper (line the base, line the sides, then line the base again to seal the lining), to prevent the mixture leaking out.

Sift the flour, cocoa powder and bicarbonate of soda into a large bowl, then add the sugar, ground almonds and salt. Make three holes in the dry mixture with a spoon. Put the vanilla in one hole, the vinegar in the second, and the oil into the third. Pour in the prune juice and mix well. Bubbles will start to rise to the surface. Pour the batter into the prepared cake tin and bake for 45 minutes to 1 hour, or until a skewer inserted into the centre of the cake comes out clean. Remove the cake from the tin and leave it to cool on a wire rack.

To make the ganache icing, blitz the chocolate into crumbs in a food processor. Place the crumbs in a heatproof glass bowl. Heat the cream to boiling point in a heavy-based saucepan, then pour the cream over the chocolate. Gently mix the chocolate with the cream, working from the centre of the bowl outwards with a rubber spatula, until you have a smooth and glossy emulsion. Let it cool to room temperature, then spread it on top of the cooled cake. If you want to keep to the vegan theme, make a Spring Water Ganache icing (see page 114).

WHITE CHOCOLATE HEARTBREAKERS

These delightful cakes came about when one of my Twitter friends, The Gentleman Baker, suggested making a white chocolate version of a classic melt-in-the-middle chocolate fondant pudding. We collaborated and re-invented the recipe. You can substitute the white chocolate for dark chocolate and try different flavours for the liquid centre, such as the saffron and cardamom ganache in the White Chocolate Mousse (see page 102).

Makes 12 heart-shaped cakes

Special equipment

2 x 6-hole silicone heart cupcake moulds (see p248 for stockists), or 12 x 80ml ramekins

12 x 15ml-hole silicone ice-cube tray

Ingredients

400g Valrhona Ivoire chips or Green & Black's white chocolate, broken into small pieces

100g softened unsalted butter, diced

3 large eggs, beaten

100g self-raising flour, sifted

1 tsp vanilla extract

A pinch of salt

100g ground almonds

For the 'surprise' centre

80g good quality white chocolate

80ml raspberry purée (if you make it at home, purée 125g of raspberries and pass them through a sieve to get rid of the seeds), at room temperature

Make the 'surprise' raspberry ganache centre the day before you need it. Melt the chocolate in a bowl over a bain-marie and stir in the raspberry purée. Pour 2 teaspoons of the mixture into each hole of the ice-cube tray and place in the freezer to set.

Preheat the oven to 190°C/gas mark 5. If you are using ramekins, base-line them with baking parchment.

Chop 200g of the white chocolate into pea-sized pieces. Melt the remaining chocolate in a bowl over a bain-marie, then add the butter and blend with a wooden spoon or stick blender until combined. Whisk in the beaten eggs, a spoon at a time, adding a teaspoonful of the flour every now and then to stop the mixture curdling. Add the vanilla extract to the chocolate mixture and whisk until light and fluffy. Gently fold in the remaining sifted flour, salt, ground almonds and 100g of the chopped chocolate. Scatter some of the remaining white chocolate in the bottom of each mould or greased and floured ramekin (enough to cover the base), then cover with about 1cm of cake mixture. Place half of one ice cube of frozen ganache in the centre of the mixture, then fill the moulds or ramekins with the remaining sponge mixture so that it covers the fruity ganache and reaches the tops of the moulds or ramekins. Place the moulds or ramekins on to a baking sheet and put them into the oven. Turn the oven temperature down to 160°C/gas mark 3 and bake the cakes for 25–30 minutes until the sponge is risen and golden and just cooked through – there should be a few sticky crumbs visible on the skewer. Leave to cool for 5 minutes before attempting to remove them from the moulds or ramekins; they are very fragile. Serve the cakes immediately, while they are still warm, so that they can be cut open to reveal the liquid white chocolate and raspberry centre. Brush the cakes with some extra melted white chocolate if you want them to be even richer and sweeter.

SPICE BISCUITS

These biscuits make a perfect crunchy accompaniment for a chocolate mousse or pudding, and the molasses gives them a sweet liquorice note. Adapt the spice according to taste; I have chosen nutmeg because it's the national spice of Grenada and I love it, but ground ginger, cinnamon, cardamom or allspice are also good. It's a great dough to have in the fridge or freezer if you have children coming for tea; they can help to roll and cut...

Makes 50 biscuits

Ingredients

400g plain flour, plus extra
for dusting

1 heaped tsp baking powder

2 tsp freshly grated nutmeg

¼ tsp ground cloves

200g softened unsalted butter

200g soft brown sugar

60g molasses or black treacle

Finely grated zest of 1 washed/
unwaxed orange or lemon

A pinch of salt

1 medium egg, beaten, at
room temperature

15ml milk, plus extra for brushing

Sift the flour, baking powder and nutmeg and cloves into a large bowl. In the bowl of an electric mixer, fitted with the paddle attachment, mix the butter, sugar, molasses or black treacle, orange or lemon zest and a pinch of salt until light and creamy (you could do this by hand with a wooden spoon), then add the sifted dry ingredients and beat them in before incorporating the egg and milk a little at a time. Gently knead the mixture on a lightly floured surface until you have soft, smooth dough. Divide the dough in half, wrap each piece in clingfilm and rest it in the fridge overnight.

Heat the oven to 150°C/gas mark 2 and line two or three large baking trays with non-stick baking paper (or use silicone trays). Let the dough soften a little, then unwrap it and roll it out on a clean and lightly floured work surface to about 5mm thick. Cut the dough into shapes with a biscuit cutter, re-kneading and rolling the trimmings to make more biscuits. You may need to re-chill the dough if it starts to become too soft. Place the shapes carefully on the prepared trays, spaced slightly apart, and chill once more until firm. Brush them with a little milk and bake in batches for 30–35 minutes, or until just beginning to darken slightly around the edges. Transfer to a wire rack to cool. Store in an airtight container for up to a week.

GRENADA CHOCOLATE BROWNIE

These are wonderfully moist, very rich and, of course, deeply darkly chocolatey.

Makes 18 small or 9 large brownies

Special equipment
18cm shallow square baking tin or silicone cake mould

Ingredients
125g pecan nuts or almonds, roughly chopped
100g Grenada Chocolate Co. dark chocolate (82% cocoa solids), broken into pieces
2 large eggs
185g golden caster sugar
185g softened unsalted butter, plus extra for greasing
75g plain flour
Icing sugar, for dusting

Preheat the oven to 160°C/gas mark 3. Grease the tin, line the base with greaseproof paper, then grease the paper (silicone moulds do not need to be lined).

Place the nuts on a baking tray and toast them in the oven for a couple of minutes, until lightly browned. Remove from the hot tray and set aside to cool. Alternatively, caramelise the nuts in sugar to make a simple praline (see page 46) and break into big pieces.

Melt the chocolate in a bowl over a bain-marie. In a large bowl whisk the eggs with the sugar until the sugar has dissolved and you have a light and fluffy mixture. The whisk should leave a ribbon trail in the mixture when lifted.

In a separate bowl, beat the butter until soft and creamy. Add the melted chocolate, mix well to combine, then stir in the egg mixture a spoonful at a time until thoroughly combined. Sift in the flour, then fold in the toasted or caramelised nuts using a rubber spatula. The texture of the mixture should be firm, like a butter cream. Pour the mixture into the prepared brownie tin or silicone mould and dust the surface of the mixture lightly with icing sugar. Bake in the oven for approximately 20–35 minutes, depending on how gooey you like your brownies. Personally I like them to be a bit undercooked, but cooked enough so that you don't get the taste of raw flour: a skewer inserted into the centre of the brownie mixture should come out with a little sticky mixture on it, not completely clean. Let the brownies cool a little in the tin before turning them out on to a wire rack. Cut into squares when cool. The brownies will keep for up to a week in an airtight container.

CHOCOLATE LACE BISCUITS

Also called tuiles dentelles, these are really simple and so delicious. Serve them after a meal or alongside a lemon posset or chocolate mousse.

Makes about 30 biscuits

Special equipment

Silicone mat (optional)

Tuile mould (optional, see p249 for stockists)

Ingredients

75g softened unsalted butter

200g icing sugar

30g plain flour

20g unsweetened cocoa powder

75ml fresh orange juice, at room temperature

Finely grated zest of 1 orange

25–30g cocoa nibs (see p249 for stockists)

Preheat the oven to 160°C/gas mark 3.

Place the butter and icing sugar in a large bowl and cream together with a wooden spoon until light and fluffy. Sift the flour and cocoa powder into the bowl and add the orange juice and zest. Mix thoroughly until smooth.

Drop teaspoons of the mixture at least 12cm apart on to baking trays lined with silicone mats or greased non-stick baking paper. Spread out the mixture thinly with a lightly wetted finger into 6cm discs or ovals. Sprinkle a few cocoa nibs on top of each one.

Bake in batches for 8 minutes, until they have spread out, there are plenty of holes in the mixture, and they are lacy around the edges. Remove from the oven and leave to cool for 1–2 minutes to firm up slightly, then one at a time carefully lift them off the mats or sheets with a palette knife while they are still warm and malleable, and place them into a tuile mould nib-side down, or shape them around a rolling pin, nib-side up. If you want basket-shaped containers, mould them over the top of a small upturned glass bowl or ramekin.

The tuiles are very sensitive to moisture, so are best made just before serving. If storing for a short while, keep them in an airtight container in a cool, dry place.

Variation: Orange almond tuiles

Follow the method above, replacing the cocoa powder with 20g extra plain flour. Sprinkle with 50g of chopped and toasted slivered almonds instead of the cocoa nibs before baking.

BILLIONAIRE'S LEMON SHORTBREAD

Millionaire's shortbread is a bit ordinary, and often made with industrial milk chocolate. This is a really high calibre version, made with Salted Lemon Caramel. If you want to gild the lily, decorate the top with edible gold leaf.

Makes about 20 fingers

Special equipment

20 x 30cm baking tray, loose-bottomed brownie tin or Swiss roll tin

Ingredients

130g softened unsalted butter, diced, plus extra for greasing

1g Fleur de Sel salt
(we use Halen Môn from Anglesey)

100g soft light brown sugar

1 tsp Ndali pure vanilla extract

40g ground almonds

1 medium egg, beaten

160g plain flour, plus extra for dusting

Scant ½ tsp baking powder

1 quantity Salted Lemon Caramel (see p31)

150g good quality dark chocolate

Edible gold leaf, to decorate
(optional, see p249 for stockists)

Place the butter, salt, sugar and vanilla in a bowl and beat with a wooden spoon until light and fluffy. Stir in the ground almonds followed by the egg. Sift in the flour with the baking powder, mix until just combined and knead lightly on a clean work surface. Wrap the dough in clingfilm and chill for a few hours, or overnight.

Preheat the oven to 150°C/gas mark 2. Unwrap the chilled dough and let it soften at room temperature for a few minutes. Place it on a lightly floured surface and roll it out to about 3cm thick. Grease the tray or tin and line it with buttered greaseproof paper, and press the mixture evenly into the tin with lightly floured fingers. Bake for 25–30 minutes or until lightly golden, and leave to cool.

Make the Salted Lemon Caramel, and pour it over the cooled shortbread, tilting the tin to cover the shortbread with an even layer of caramel. Leave it to set overnight in the fridge before melting or tempering the chocolate (see page 226) and spreading it over the caramel layer.

Cut into rectangles and decorate with edible gold leaf, if desired. To make gold leaf 'stick', and to stop it flying away, use a hot, dry teaspoon to melt a tiny patch on the set chocolate before applying the gold leaf with a paint brush.

POWER
GRANOLA

A healthy way to start the day, this low GI (glycaemic index) recipe releases energy slowly into the bloodstream and is full of protein, vitamins, essential fatty acids and fibre. Enjoy it with plain yoghurt and fresh or poached fruit. I like to add green barley grass powder to mine. It's an acquired taste, but definitely sits in the 'super food' category. The cocoa nibs give the granola a lovely crunch and a delicate chocolate flavour.

Makes 750g

Ingredients

100ml grapeseed oil, plus extra
for greasing

90g honey

100g light tahini paste

200g rolled oats

50g flaked almonds

100g ground seeds, eg. pumpkin,
sunflower, flax, sesame and
linseeds (you can buy ready
ground seeds in health food
shops)

50g goji berries

50g cocoa nibs

Green barley grass powder,
to serve (optional, see p249 for
stockists)

Preheat the oven to 180°C/gas mark 4, and lightly grease two large baking trays.

Warm the oil, honey and tahini in a saucepan over a gentle heat, stirring to mix, then add the oats, almonds, ground seeds, goji berries and cocoa nibs. Stir well and divide the mixture evenly between the two baking trays. Bake into the oven for 10 minutes. Remove and cool on the tray, then store in an airtight container. Sprinkle a few teaspoons of barley grass powder over the granola just before serving, if desired. The granola will keep for up to two weeks.

CHOCOLATE BRIOCHE

This wonderfully rich and buttery brioche is worth the effort. Though you need to make the dough a day before baking it, it is much better than anything you can buy – it would sell a house if anyone viewed it when you were baking them! You'll notice that the quantity of eggs is provided in grams: this is a more accurate measure, essential for this recipe.

Makes 12 individual brioches

Special equipment
12 individual brioche tins
(9cm across the top)

Ingredients
330g strong plain white flour, '00' if possible, plus extra for dusting

5g fine salt

15g fresh yeast, finely crumbled or 7g dried easy-blend yeast

50g caster sugar

200g eggs, beaten, plus extra for glazing (weigh, after discarding shell, into a bowl set on digital scales)

200g chilled unsalted butter, cut into 1cm pieces, plus extra for greasing

1 tbsp orange-flower water (optional)

50–75g Grenada Chocolate Co. chocolate (71% cocoa solids), broken into squares

granulated sugar, for sprinkling

Sift the flour and salt into the large bowl of a free-standing food mixer fitted with a dough hook attachment, and add the yeast, sugar and eggs. Mix on low speed for about 10 minutes, or until you have a smooth silky mixture, then gradually add the cold butter, a few pieces at a time, and mix until soft and well combined. (Making the dough with an electric mixer results in a light and airy brioche, as the butter doesn't melt into the dough.)

Add the orange-flower water, if using, and mix the dough on medium speed for a further 2 minutes. Don't be alarmed if the dough seems rather sticky. Remove the bowl from the mixer, cover it with clingfilm and leave it in a warm place for 1 hour. Remove the clingfilm and return the bowl to the mixer. Mix on low speed for 1 minute to knock it back. Re-cover and place the bowl of dough in the fridge for at least 12 hours (preferably overnight).

The next day, lightly grease and flour the brioche tins. Remove the dough from the fridge, scoop it out of the bowl on to a lightly floured work surface. You should have about 800g of dough, which will now feel very firm, as the butter will have hardened in the fridge. Divide the dough into 12 equal pieces, weighing about 65g each, to fit your tins. Shape the pieces of dough into balls on a lightly floured surface, burying 1 chocolate square in the centre of each ball. Place the dough pieces seam side down in the prepared tins. Leave them in a warm place, covered with a clean damp cloth, to rise until they increase in size by at least a third and become light and airy. This can take 1–2 hours, or you can leave them in the fridge overnight and the brioche will be ready to bake after being brought back to room temperature in the morning.

Preheat the oven to 190°C/gas
mark 5. Brush the tops of each
brioche lightly with beaten egg
and place the tins on a baking tray.
Bake for 5–10 minutes, until lightly
coloured, then reduce the heat to
170°C/gas mark 3 and bake them
for a further 5–10 minutes, or until
they sound hollow when tapped on
the bottom and are golden brown.
Turn out and serve immediately
while they are still warm, or leave
them to cool on a wire rack.

GRENADA RUM CAKE

This cake looks a bit like Parkin. It is delicate and moist, and not too sweet, and my sister says 'one slice is never enough'. It keeps well, too, and you can make it up to three days in advance. The quantity of rum you choose to add to the syrup will determine whether it contributes a subtle flavour or a bit of a kick.

Serves 20–30

Special equipment

23 x 30cm 6–7cm
rectangular cake tin

Ingredients

120g raisins

4 tbsp dark rum

6 medium eggs

220g golden caster sugar

240g ground almonds

140g plain flour

50g cocoa powder

12g baking powder

300ml milk

250g Grenada Chocolate Co.
chocolate (60–71% cocoa solids),
broken into pieces

280g well softened unsalted butter,
plus extra for greasing

For the syrup

125g golden caster sugar

125ml water

Pared zest of ½ small lemon

1 tsp fresh lemon juice

2½ tbsp dark rum

¼ tsp fine freshly grated nutmeg

Day 1: place the raisins in a bowl and spoon over the rum. Leave to soak overnight. Make the syrup: dissolve the sugar and water in a small saucepan over a low heat. Add lemon zest and boil for 5 minutes. Remove the pan from the heat and add the lemon juice, rum and grated nutmeg. Leave overnight.

Day 2: lightly grease the tin with butter and line it with greaseproof paper. Put the eggs and sugar into a large bowl. Beat with an electric hand whisk until the mixture is pale and thick enough to leave a trail when the whisk is lifted out, then fold in the ground almonds and soaked raisins and rum. In a separate bowl mix together the flour, cocoa powder and baking powder. Sift half of the dry ingredients into the wet egg and almond mixture, mix gently, then pour in half the milk, mix again, then sift in the remaining dry ingredients, stirring, followed by the rest of the milk.

Preheat the oven to 160°C/gas mark 3. Melt the chocolate in a bowl over a bain-marie. Remove the bowl from the bain-marie and stir in a fifth of the cake mixture, mixing thoroughly. Gradually add the rest of the mixture, a little at a time, stirring until combined.

In a separate bowl beat the butter until pale and fluffy, then briskly beat it into the cake mixture. Spoon the mixture into the prepared tin and bake for 40-45 minutes, or until a skewer inserted into the centre of the cake comes out with just a few sticky crumbs attached. Remove the cake from the oven and spike the top with a fine needle. Strain the syrup and while the cake is still warm, slowly spoon the syrup over the cake, letting it soak in. Leave to cool in the tin for an hour, then turn out and leave to cool completely on a wire rack. Serve with Chantilly cream, laced with rum if you desire.

SAVOURY CHOCO —LATE

As tomato ketchup, mango chutney, redcurrant jelly and plum sauce are all commonly accepted condiments for savoury foods, why do so many people throw up their hands in horror at the idea of using chocolate in savoury recipes? There is a long history of mixing sweet ingredients with savoury. Just consider Middle Eastern, Thai, Chinese and Sicilian cuisines: fine examples of culinary traditions whose 'agro dolce' dishes are much loved and transcend geographical boundaries. When I add chocolate to a savoury recipe it is to bring an extra dimension of depth and flavour to the dish, and sometimes a hint of sweetness. You can use sweetened chocolate, unsweetened cocoa or Chocolate Balsamic Glaze (see page 197).

Some of the recipes in this chapter are classics from the chocolate and savoury repertoire; others are treatments I have given to my favourite savoury dishes that are ripe for conversion. Try bringing a touch of alchemy to your dishes — you can always keep it a secret, and see if friends and family guess what the special ingredient is.

EXTREME CANAPÉS

Some of these chocolate and cheese combinations may sound avant garde, but think of parmesan and pear, manchego and quince paste, port and cheese, and then consider the nature of cheese and chocolate. Both are fermented to achieve their complex and stimulating flavour profiles, so naturally sit well together.

milk chocolate sea salt wafer and fresh goat's cheese

dark chocolate passion fruit wafer and taleggio

dark chocolate mint wafer and pecorino

dark chocolate ginger wafer and feta cheese

dark chocolate wafer and Stilton

dark chocolate wafer and camembert

You can add zested lemon and cracked pepper to the fresh goat's cheese to add an extra dimension.

CHOCOLATE BALSAMIC GLAZE

This simple little invention is an invaluable store cupboard ingredient, a thick treacly condiment with a subtle taste of chocolate. Use it in salad dressings, gravies and sauces and to deglaze roasting pans. It lends itself equally well to sweet dishes – just try it drizzled over fresh strawberries.

Makes 150ml

Ingredients

30g good quality dark chocolate, chopped into small pieces

100g caster sugar

100ml balsamic vinegar

Put the chopped chocolate into a suitable jug or small bowl for use with a stick blender.

Put the sugar and balsamic vinegar in a small saucepan and leave over a low heat until the sugar has completely dissolved. Then increase the heat, quickly bring up to the boil and immediately pour the syrup over the chocolate. Leave it to melt for 2 minutes, then blitz with the stick blender until you have a smooth and glossy emulsion. It should have the texture of molasses, and will thicken further as it cools.

Pour the glaze immediately into a clean jar, seal and label. The glaze keeps well for up to 6 months in a cool, dark place.

Make larger quantities and store in pretty wide-necked bottles or small jars; it makes a great gift.

Try experimenting with flavours, such as chilli or spices (cardamom, fennel seed and rosemary are good).

Variation: Turkey and bacon sandwich with chocolate balsamic glaze

What better way to use up leftover Christmas turkey? The chocolate balsamic glaze is much like a brown sauce, adding a sweet and sour taste.

Grill a couple of slices of your favourite bacon. Assemble the sandwich with two plain or toasted slices of sourdough bread, a handful of salad leaves, some leftover slices of white turkey meat or a grilled and sliced turkey breast, the grilled bacon, and a drizzle of glaze over the meat. Adjust seasoning to taste.

ARMENIAN LAMB

This is one of my mother-in-law Beryl's standby dishes, much loved by all the family. I have given it the chocolate treatment, which emphasises the richness and deepens the flavour, and even managed to sneak it past my children without them noticing.

Serves 4

Ingredients

1 tsp cumin seeds

½ tsp ground allspice

1 large red pepper, deseeded, and sliced into long thin strips

2 tbsp good quality olive oil

25g butter

600g lamb neck fillets, each cut into 5 large cubes, or cubed shoulder or leg meat

1 large onion, peeled and finely chopped

1 garlic clove, peeled and finely chopped

2 tsp plain flour

1 tsp unsweetened cocoa powder

500ml lamb or chicken stock

1 tbsp tomato purée

Juice of half a lemon

1 tbsp redcurrant jelly

2–3 tbsp sour cream or crème fraîche

Salt and freshly ground black pepper

Toast the cumin seeds and allspice in a large, dry frying pan for about 1 minute, remove and set to one side. Fry the red pepper in the same dry pan for about 5 minutes, until softened and lightly browned, then set aside.

Heat the oil and butter in the pan until the butter is foaming, then add the meat and brown it on all sides. Add the red pepper, spices, onion and garlic, season with salt and pepper, and cook for about 5 minutes, then place the flour and cocoa in a sieve and dust it over the dish. Cook for another minute, then stir in the stock, tomato purée, lemon juice and redcurrant jelly. Simmer gently, uncovered, stirring occasionally, for 1 hour or until the meat is tender and the sauce has reduced and thickened.

Check the seasoning and adjust if necessary, then stir in the sour cream or crème fraîche just before serving. Serve with plain basmati rice or couscous and a refreshing salad – we love a salad of fennel, chicory and pomegranate seeds dressed with a fresh lemon or lime vinaigrette.

LAPIN A LA MOUTARDE WITH CHOCOLATE

This is a French classic with a chocolate twist. Rabbit is one of my favourite meats, and cooked this way it is supremely tender and delicate. I always choose wild rabbit, a highly sustainable organic meat.

Serves 6–8

Ingredients

1.75kg whole wild rabbit, jointed into 10 pieces (ask your butcher to prepare the rabbit for you)

4 tbsp plain flour, seasoned with salt and freshly ground black pepper

1 tbsp unsalted butter

2 tbsp olive oil

12 small shallots, peeled and left whole

300g fennel bulb, trimmed and cut into 16 wedges

200g carrots, peeled and cut into quarters lengthways

120ml glass of dry white wine

400ml chicken stock or water

25g good quality dark chocolate (minimum 70% cocoa solids)

2–3 tbsp Dijon mustard

3 tbsp crème fraîche

Dust the rabbit pieces in the seasoned flour, shaking off any excess. Heat the butter with the oil in a skillet or heavy-based frying pan until foaming, and brown the meat on all sides (you may need to do this in batches, depending on the size of your pan; you don't want to over-crowd the pan and steam the meat). Remove the meat with a slotted spoon, and transfer it to a casserole or wide heavy-based sauté pan. Brown the whole shallots in the same frying pan or skillet, then add them to the meat with the fennel and carrots, and cook, stirring, over a low heat for a couple of minutes. Add the wine, bring to a simmer and add just enough water or stock to cover. Part-cover and cook over a low heat for 1 hour, or until the rabbit is tender. Just before serving, turn off the heat, stir in the chocolate, allowing it to melt, and add the mustard and crème fraîche. Season to taste and serve with mashed potatoes or tagliatelle.

KHORESHT FESENJAN

*One of my earliest memories of food is watching my mother making Persian dishes.
I adore Persian cuisine now, as I did then, and this sweet and sour chicken stew is
particularly memorable. The cocoa nibs give it a lovely extra crunch and depth of flavour.*

Serves 6–8

Ingredients

3 tbsp butter

3 tbsp olive oil

1.5 kg chicken, skinned, boned and cut into large chunks (keep the wing joints on the bone) or 1 kg chicken breasts, cut into large chunks

1 large onion, peeled and finely chopped

20g tomato purée

80g cocoa nibs (see p248 for stockists)

50g shelled walnuts, chopped

500ml water, or chicken or vegetable stock

1 tsp salt

1 tbsp caster sugar

½ tsp ground cinnamon

2 tbsp lemon juice

2–3 tbsp pomegranate molasses, according to taste

Melt the butter with the oil in a large heavy-based lidded saucepan. Add the chicken pieces and fry until browned all over, then remove them with a slotted spoon and set aside. Put the onion in the pan and cook until soft and lightly browned. Add the tomato purée, cocoa nibs and walnuts, and cook for a few minutes. Add the water or stock, salt, sugar, cinnamon, lemon juice and pomegranate molasses, adjust the seasoning and stir well. Return the chicken to the pan and cover. Simmer over a low heat for 45 minutes, or until the chicken is tender. Serve with chelo (Persian rice) or plain basmati rice.

CHOCOLATE TEMPURA OYSTERS

I loved fresh oysters until I developed an allergy to them, but I can eat cooked ones and this is a lovely dish we occasionally make at Christmas, to enjoy with a glass of champagne. I've modified Rick Stein's tempura batter recipe, adding cocoa nibs and a touch of herbs and spice.

Serves 4

Ingredients

20–24 large oysters

1–1.5 litres sunflower or vegetable oil, for deep-frying

For the batter

50g plain flour

50g cornflour

A small pinch of salt

1 medium-hot red chilli, seeded and very finely chopped

50g cocoa nibs (see p248 for stockists)

1 tbsp finely chopped fresh coriander

175ml ice-cold soda water, from a new bottle

For the chocolate dipping sauce

1 tbsp dark soy sauce

4 tbsp sake

2 tbsp Chocolate Balsamic Glaze (see page 197)

1 tbsp finely chopped fresh root ginger

To serve

100g piece of peeled daikon, finely grated

Wasabi paste, to taste

Fresh coriander sprigs, to garnish

Heat some oil for deep-frying to 190°C. Mix together the ingredients for the dipping sauce and divide it between 4 dipping saucers. Arrange the grated daikon in a little pile on each serving plate.

Open the oysters and release them from their shells. Drain the meats briefly on kitchen paper and dry the deepest shells for serving.

Make the batter by sifting the flour, cornflour and salt into a small mixing bowl. Stir in the red chilli, cocoa nibs and chopped coriander, then quickly stir in the soda water (with chopsticks if you have some to hand) until only just mixed in but still a little lumpy.

Drop the oysters into the batter four at a time and then lift them out, trying to take some of the cocoa nibs and chilli from the batter with each one. Drop the oysters into the hot oil and deep-fry for 1½ minutes until crisp and very lightly golden. Remove with a slotted spoon and drain briefly on plenty of kitchen paper.

Return the cooked oysters to their shells, arrange each shell on each plate and garnish with the coriander sprigs. Serve immediately with the dipping sauce and grated daikon.

Note: Cooking oysters kills harmful bacteria tht can be present in raw oysters.

CITRUS-BRAISED FENNEL WITH WHITE CHOCOLATE

This is a surprisingly subtle and aromatic dish, an ideal accompaniment for roast meat, duck or game, or simply great eaten by itself between courses or at the end of a meal. It is delicately sweet, with a meltingly-soft texture and a touch of acidity. Endive makes a delicious alternative to fennel.

Serves 4

Ingredients

25g unsalted butter

25g good quality white chocolate

2 large bulbs of Florence fennel, cut into quarters lengthways through the root end (so that the pieces stay together in wedges)

Juice of 1 large orange (approximately 100ml)

1 tbsp freshly squeezed lemon juice

Salt and freshly ground black pepper

Melt the butter over a gentle heat in a large skillet or heavy-based frying pan with a tight-fitting lid. Add the white chocolate and let it melt slowly, then stir it into the butter.

Place the fennel wedges cut-side down in the pan, and leave them to brown over a low heat for 6–7 minutes. Turn on to the other cut face and repeat, then turn the pieces on to their backs and pour over the orange and lemon juice and season with a little salt and pepper.

Cover and gently braise for about 25 minutes, until the fennel is cooked through and the juices have caramelised slightly and formed a thick and syrupy sauce. Adjust the seasoning to taste and serve immediately.

GRENADA PEPPERPOT

We often eat pepperpot stew at Shadel Nyack Compton's restaurant on the Belmont Estate when we visit our Grococo farm in Grenada. I have based this recipe on one from Wendy Hartland's Great Caribbean Recipes from Belmont Estate, *and given it a chocolate twist. Traditionally the pepperpot was literally passed down through generations in its special clay pot, used only for this dish, which would sit over a charcoal brazier and be added to every day and re-boiled. Cassareep, the fermented juice of the cassava root, acts as a preservative, but don't worry if you can't source it. It is not a formal dish, so vary the meat and spices as you wish. The flavour develops the longer it's kept.*

Serves 12

Special equipment
Clay pot or large lidded casserole

Ingredients
1.5 kg of meat, which can include any of the following: cow heel or pig's trotter (cut in half), chunks of oxtail, stewing steak or brisket, sliced belly pork
50 ml cassareep (optional)
1–2 Scotch bonnet chillies, finely chopped, to taste
1 onion, peeled and roughly chopped
2 garlic cloves, peeled and finely chopped
Juice of 1 lime
Juice of 1 lemon
Thumb-size piece of fresh ginger, peeled and grated
1 tbsp tomato purée (optional)
Handful of thyme leaves and chopped chives
1 tsp salt, or to taste
10g Grenada Chocolate Co. dark chocolate, chopped
salt and freshly ground black pepper

Cut the meat into large 5 cm chunks, season and brown, in batches if necessary, in the clay pot or casserole. Add the rest of the ingredients (except the chocolate), including the teaspoon of salt, cover with approximately 1.5 litres of water and bring to the boil. Cover with a lid and cook gently for 3 hours or until the meat is tender. Stir in the chocolate at the end of the cooking time, then simmer for another 15 minutes. Adjust seasoning and serve with white rice or bread.

Note: You can find cassareep in bottles in ethnic food stores.

OLIVE CHOCOLATE TAPENADE

I love this recipe. It's so easy to make and is full of great umami flavours. Tapenade is often soft and oily in texture, but here the addition of chocolate gives it a welcome firmness and a texture resembling meat terrine. Serve it on crostini with fresh goat's cheese, as a dip for crudités – thin wedges of raw fennel or celery work well – or spread it over the pastry base of a tomato tart.

Makes enough to fill a 450g jar

Ingredients

1 x 290–300g jar of Kalamata olives (or another black variety), pitted (190g drained weight)

5 preserved anchovy fillets, drained and chopped

1 large garlic clove, peeled and chopped

2 tbsp capers, squeezed of vinegar

5 tbsp good quality olive oil, plus more for jarring

1 fresh red chilli, deseeded and thinly sliced, or to taste

2 tbsp rum (optional)

25g good quality dark chocolate

Pulse all of the ingredients except the chocolate in a food processor until they have formed a rough paste. Melt the chocolate in a bowl over a bain-marie, and stir it into the tapenade. If you don't plan to use the tapenade immediately, press it into a sterilised jar and cover it with a layer of olive oil before sealing. It will keep well in the fridge for at least 2 weeks.

Mott loves to make this recipe, as he is pescetarian – he eats fish. He uses the 100% Cocoa Grenada chocolate and adds 40g of it to give that firm texture.

JAPANESE PUMPKIN NIMONO

This is one of my husband James's classic dishes that everyone loves, even those who say they don't like pumpkin. You can use butternut squash, though the flesh falls apart rapidly, whereas the traditional Kabocha keeps its shape. The nutty pumpkin seed oil is fantastic stuff and the chocolate adds a playful twist.

Serves 6

Ingredients

half a 1.2kg Kabocha pumpkin, deseeded and cut into thin wedges or bite-sized pieces (skin on – peel if using butternut squash)

3 tbsp cold-pressed pumpkin seed oil (alternatively walnut, hazelnut, or 1 tbsp sesame mixed with 3 tbsp sunflower oil)

50ml light soy sauce

120ml dry white wine

30g good quality milk chocolate, broken into small pieces

Place the pumpkin flesh in a large heavy-based saucepan with the oil and cook over a medium heat for a minute or two until lightly browned, then add the soy sauce and wine. Continue to cook, covered, for about 20 minutes, or until the pumpkin is tender and the liquid has reduced by half.

Just before serving, turn off the heat, add the chocolate pieces to the pan, let them melt into the sauce, and stir. Serve with grilled fish, spinach or mustard greens, and some wasabi or horseradish sauce on the side, or as a vegetable side dish with a traditional roast.

SAVOURY CHOCO— LATE BISCUITS

I met Vanessa Kimbell when she visited our shop to learn about chocolate for her cook-book, Prepped, *and this is one of her inspired recipes. Chocolate and cheese may seem unlikely bedfellows, but on reflection they are surprisingly similar, in that they both require fermentation to bring out their complex flavour profiles (we sometimes serve chocolate and cheese together as 'extreme canapés', see page 194). The biscuit has a shortbread quality to it; short and crumbly before melting into a sublime combination of buttery dark, salted chocolate with just a hint of heat. Served with mellow Cheddar, they are quite simply moreish. Freeze half of the dough if you don't want to bake all the biscuits at once.*

Makes about 25 biscuits

Ingredients

220g plain flour

½ tsp smoked paprika

4 tbsp unsweetened cocoa powder

1 tsp baking powder

60g good quality dark chocolate (70% cocoa solids), grated

2 tbsp of cardamom-infused sugar (caster sugar and a couple of bashed cardamom pods left for 6 weeks in a sealed jar)

A pinch of sea salt

145g chilled unsalted butter, diced

2 medium eggs

35g poppy seeds

Sift the flour, paprika, cocoa powder and baking powder into a bowl. Stir in the grated chocolate, sugar and salt. Rub in the butter until the mixture resembles breadcrumbs, then add 1 egg and mix to form a soft dough.

Roll the dough into a large sausage, about 5cm thick, on a well-floured surface. Beat the second egg and brush the sausage with a little of it before rolling the log on a tray covered with the poppy seeds. Wrap the log in clingfilm. Transfer the log to the fridge for an hour to chill.

Preheat the oven to 160°C/gas mark 3. Unwrap the log and, using a sharp knife, slice the log into 4–5mm-thick discs and put the discs, spaced apart, on to a large baking tray lined with non-stick baking paper. Bake for about 15 minutes, but don't be tempted to overdo them. They will become firm and crumbly when they are cool. Leave to cool on the tray, then store in an airtight container for up to a week.

Wrap the biscuits in greaseproof paper with a beautiful hunk of Cheddar to make a cracking gift for cheese-lovers.

Variation: Chilli-chocolate biscuits

To transform the biscuits into sweet chilli-chocolate biscuits, add 75g of caster sugar and chilli pepper to taste, and increase the butter by 20g.

WINES & SPIRITS WITH CHOCOLATE

There are many parallels between wine- and chocolate-making: both wine and chocolate have notable varietals with distinctive flavour profiles, both are affected by terroir and weather conditions, both are fermented and both are naturally high in tannins. The tannic qualities in chocolate and wine can cause them to clash, so what I look for when 'match-making' is low tannins and softness, the secret to a perfect lasting marriage of flavours. Older wines usually have a softer mouthfeel, and a high quality well made chocolate will be less acidic than an inferior chocolate.

The more alcohol by volume in the wine, the easier it is to find a match. Traditionally ports and dessert wines work well, and there are lots of wonderful rums, brandies and whiskies that work their magic, too.

Milk or white chocolate is generally easier to pair than dark; the perfect marriage of dark chocolate and wine remains something of a Holy Grail. I have tried so many combinations over the last 25 years, and I am still searching for a fairytale combination: a fine excuse for us all to keep on trying different combinations.

HOLDING YOUR OWN CHOCOLATE TASTING SESSION AT HOME

Invite a few friends for a simple supper, as it's best to eat something savoury before launching into a chocolate tasting (and, of course, it is the natural dessert course if you don't have time to make a pudding).

Ask everyone to bring their favourite chocolate bar, or you could choose the bars yourself. I recommend tasting across the price range and cocoa percentage range. Six types of chocolate are probably enough, and the same or fewer wines or spirits.

Depending how serious you want to get, you can provide paper for people to jot down their observations.

Smell the chocolate and the wine or spirit independently before tasting them. Try a small piece of chocolate, letting the taste linger, before sipping the wine or spirit. Notice how the alcohol amplifies or deadens the flavour notes of the chocolate. Try the wine by itself and see if the chocolate enhances it or not. For a scholarly tasting, offer cups of white tea to cleanse the palate between pairings, made with water that is not quite boiling (85°C), or room temperature water. Tea also sharpens the mind and senses, and lets the chocolate notes shine through.

WINES

White

Chocolate-friendly white wines range from dessert and fortified wines such as Tokaji, Sauternes, Monbazillac and Muscat (Baumes de Venise), vins jaunes such as Jurançon, drier wines like Picpoul de Pinet or wines from Alsace, Germany and their New World equivalents such as Gewürztraminer. Here is a selection of wines and chocolates that have been paired particularly successfully:

— Rococo Sea Salt Artisan bar with Picpoul de Pinet Chateau de la Mirande '03 or De Bortoli PHI Chardonnay
— Rococo Cardamom and White Chocolate Artisan bar with Domaine de Tariquet, 1er Grives 'Gros Manseng' '02
— Grenada Chocolate Co. 60% dark chocolate with Jurancon Magendia 'Clos Lapeyre' Petit Manseng '00
— Grenada Chocolate Co. 71% dark chocolate with Coteaux de Layon 'St. Lambert' Dom Ognereau

Red

Pair red wines with dark chocolate. Our Grenada bars and Artisan bars (Violet, Basil and Lime, Chilli, Orange Confit) are beautiful pairings, as is Valrhona Manjari. Heavy reds such as cabernet sauvignon, Grenache and syrah pair well, as does a sparkling shiraz, a pinot noir, or a sweet red such as Banyuls. Lower tannins tend to work better. Here is a selection of wines and chocolates that pair particularly well:

— Rococo Candied Orange and Dark Chocolate Artisan bar with Banyuls 'Clos de Paulilles' Rimage '03
— Valrhona Guanaja with Bourgeuil les Vingts Lieux Dits 'Gamay-Pinot Noir' '02
— Akesson's Black Peppercorn bar with Sud Absolu, Cotes du Ventoux 'Grenache, Syrah' '03

Rosé

It sounds a bit of a cliché, but rosé wines and champagnes go very well with rose-scented chocolate, particularly our milk chocolate Rose Otto Artisan bar. Our Sea Salt milk chocolate and cardamom bars also work well with the fruity rosés from the South of France, particularly Provence. Try this winning combination:

— Rococo Milk Chocolate Rose Otto Artisan bar with Devaux Rose Champagne NV

Sparkling

Romantics often say that chocolate and champagne make a great pair, and it's certainly fun trying it out. However, champagne often overpowers chocolate, though there are some notable exceptions such as the pairing of our milk chocolate Rose Otto Artisan bar with a demi-sec champagne (see rosé, above) or prosecco. Try this winning combination:

— Cardamom and White Chocolate Artisan bar with Champagne Nocturne Sec NV, Taittinger

Port

Port marries most successfully with dark chocolate, and the most appealing matches are with nutty, spicy or citrussy chocolates. Here is a selection of chocolates and ports that pair particularly well:

— Chocolate Dipped Candied Peel (see page 63) with Taylor's 10-yr-old tawny
— Grenada Chocolate Co. 60% dark chocolate with Fonseca Bin 27
— Grenada Chocolate Co. 65% dark chocolate with Taylor's 1999 LBV
— Valrhona Manjari No 1 Grand Cru 64% dark chocolate with Taylor's Quinta de Vargellas
— Caramelised Almond Rococo 65% chocolate with Fonseca Guimaraens Vintage 1986
— Red berry fruit ganache from the Rococo Couture Collection with Noval LBV

Sherry

Sherries are one of the unsung heroes of the drinks cabinet, often derided as being a sweet drink suitable for the vicar's wife or mother-in-law. In fact there are some wonderful complex vintages out there, made with great care, which match beautifully with chocolate (or tapas, for that matter). We have suggested some sweet and dry sherries here, which were a hit when we held a chocolate and sherry tasting with food writer and lover of sherry Kevin Gould.

— Valrhona Caraibe and Grenada Chocolate Co. with Gonzalez Byass Tio Pepe Fino
— Rococo's Sea Salt Artisan bar with Perez Marin La Guita Manzanilla
— Rococo's Almond or Nutmeg Artisan bar with Valdespino Tio Diego Amontillado
— Rococo's Geranium Artisan bar with Gonzalez Byass Palo Cortado Apostoles
— Rococo's Classic Truffles (see page 26) with Osborne Bailen Oloroso
— Valrhona Guananja with Osborne Pedro Ximenez Viejo

SPIRITS

Rum

Rum and chocolate are a match made in heaven. I have held tastings with the Rum Ambassador Ian Burrell who knows his rums inside out, and these were our favourite combinations. As with sherry, aged rum is much more wallet-friendly than aged whiskies or ports.

— White Cardamom Artisan bar with Sailor Jerry Spiced Rum
— Grenada Chocolate Co. 71% dark chocolate or Guanaja with Havana Club Especial
— Mango and Passion Fruit Rococo ganache with El Dorado or Cockspur
— Akesson's Black Pepper chocolate with Angostura 1824 Reserve Rum from Trinidad and Tobago
— Rococo Rose Wafer with Elements Eight Spiced Rum

Malt whiskies

Single malts work beautifully with chocolate. In fact, you can pair most whiskies with chocolate. Smoky and peaty whiskies work particularly well with our Grenada dark chocolate bars; personally, I love whiskies from the island of Islay, particularly Bruichladdich, Bowmore, Laphroaig, Ardbeg, Lagavulin and Caol Ila.

EQUIP—MENT, TECH—NIQUES, INGRE—DIENTS

BATTERIE
DE CUISINE

You can spend thousands of pounds on expensive chocolate-making equipment, but to make chocolates on a domestic scale there are just a few simple pieces of kit that we recommend to home cooks (and I've thrown in a few well-loved gadgets for good measure).

— **Heatproof bowl** or **bain-marie**

— **Marble slab**

— **Silicone mats**

— **Wire rack**

— **Dipping forks**

— **Electric hand whisk**

— **Thermometers**: A pricier digital thermometer is useful for ganaches and tempering, as it's that little bit more accurate, but a glass probe thermometer is fine for making confectionery. An oven thermometer is a useful tool if you are a keen baker, as thermostats on domestic ovens are notoriously inaccurate.

— **Stepped pallet knife**

— **Triangular scraper**

— **Flexible rubber spatula**

— **Free-standing food mixer**

— **Stick blender**: Invest in a more expensive brand, which will have a more robust motor and blades and will last for years.

— **Food processor**: You need one with a powerful motor, so invest in the best.

— **Tabletop tempering machine**: Ideal for small amounts of chocolate. We have had ours for 20 years and it's still going strong (see p246 for stockists).

— **Thermomix**: This is an expensive piece of kit, granted, but it is a wonderful tool for the enthusiastic home cook, and a darling of every Michelin-starred kitchen. Its uses are endless: chopping, steaming, making mayonnaise, hollandaise, doughs, pastries and granitas. I love mine.

— **Disposable piping bags** and a set of nozzles.

— **Digital scales** with 1g graduations.

MELT —ING CHOC— OLATE

There are a number of ways to melt chocolate and a few pitfalls, too. Follow one of the three methods outlined here, and melt the chocolate slowly. The main things to avoid are water getting into the chocolate and the chocolate overheating. You can cool and re-melt the chocolate several times if you handle it carefully. If you are planning to temper the chocolate (see Tempering, page 226–228), you may find you need to practise melting it a few times until you get the feel for it. I prefer to use a very low oven to melt chocolate, but the bain-marie and microwave methods work well, too.

Bear in mind that white and milk chocolate have a lower melting point than dark chocolate (see page 242).

BAIN-MARIE METHOD

This quick and simple method involves melting the chocolate over boiling water. If you are melting a bar or slab of chocolate, break it into squares or roughly chop it before placing it in the bowl. Make sure the heatproof bowl into which you place your chocolate is bigger than the pan of water, so you can seal off the water (this avoids steam getting into the chocolate and ruining it). You should need only a couple of inches of water in the pan, and the bottom of the bowl should not touch the water. Turn off the heat when the water reaches boiling point, then add the chocolate to the suspended bowl. The residual heat should melt the chocolate. If it doesn't, put the pan of water back over a low heat for a short time to warm it up again. If you take the bowl off the water, dry the bottom of the bowl with a tea towel to avoid any water getting into the melted chocolate.

OVEN METHOD

Though slower than the bain-marie method, this process has many advantages: no water or moisture is involved, the risk of the chocolate burning is lower, and you can keep the chocolate warm for longer. Most pastry chefs and chocolatiers have 'warm cupboards', which are kept at around 50°C. Some of you may be lucky enough to have one in your kitchen. If not, set your oven to its lowest setting, place roughly broken chocolate in a shallow ovenproof dish and leave it in the oven for 10–15 minutes until the chocolate has melted. It may look like it has not melted, as chocolate often holds its form when soft, so prod it with a spoon to see if it collapses. Give it a stir and it is ready for use.

MICROWAVE METHOD

This is my least favourite method, especially as I don't have a microwave in my house. However, many chefs do like to use them for melting chocolate and it works well as long as you don't use a high setting or heat it for too long. The lack of water, which spoils melting chocolate, is also an advantage. Place small pieces of chocolate, in a microwaveable glass or plastic bowl. Melt the chocolate on short bursts, 30 seconds to 1 minute, and keep checking and stirring the chocolate to make sure it doesn't burn.

To use melted chocolate for tempering (see page 226), the chocolate must be completely melted. To use it for ganaches you will be adding hot cream, so it won't matter too much if it is not completely melted.

TEM— PERING

Tempering is the perfect alignment of the cocoa butter crystals in chocolate. Cocoa butter is intrinsically unstable and unpredictable: tempering stabilises the 'good' crystals. The process involves melting, cooling and moving the chocolate to create an orderly structure of crystals, resulting in well behaved chocolate that will do what you want it to do: set quickly, contract away from the surface of a mould and give you shiny, crisp chocolate.

Tempered chocolate...

— keeps its shine
— gives an audible 'snap' when broken
— melts evenly, resulting in a smooth, silky mouth-feel
— shrinks from moulds, facilitating removal
— gives stability and longer life to chocolates
— prevents 'blooming' (of the cocoa butter)

I often compare the process of tempering to the activity in a school playground. The children are dropped off, and some are so eager that they start to line up. Others run around and bump into each other. It is a noisy place, full of random activity, just like the melted chocolate with the cocoa butter crystals fluidly circulating. The sound of a bell or whistle signals that it's time to stop play and line up ready for the school day. A line of children starts to take shape and order emerges from the chaos. Sometimes cajoling from peers or teachers is necessary, and one child may refuse to play ball and upset the order. The stage when the children form a quiet orderly line is what happens when the cocoa crystals are cooled and moved around, allowing perfect stable chains to form. The chocolate is quite literally *well tempered*, and when the *rogue* crystals upset the natural order it is badly tempered, and the chocolate is impossible to work with.

Couverture is the professional benchmark for chocolate that contains 32–39% cocoa butter. Many good quality bars of chocolate are made from couverture of this quality, although it is hard to ascertain the percentage of cocoa butter from the ingredients list. High cocoa solids do not guarantee high cocoa butter, strange as this may sound, and some cooking chocolates are made with non-cocoa butter-fats or oils, and should be avoided. If chocolate is labelled couverture you know you will be able to temper it, though don't confuse *couverture* with 'covering chocolate', which often contains vegetable fat.

This is a guide for the correct tempering temperatures. Though there is some leeway, because different chocolates behave in different ways, the main principles remain the same; dark chocolate can be heated to a higher temperature than milk or white, as it does not contain casein, or milk protein.

TEMPERING TEMPERATURE GUIDE

Chocolate type	Melting	Cooling	Tempered**
Dark	50–55°C	28–29°C	31–32°C
Milk	45–50°C*	27–28°C	30–31°C
White	45–50°C*	26–27°C	29–30°C

* Never heat milk or white chocolate to more than 50°C, otherwise you will denature the casein (milk proteins) that these chocolates contain. There will be grainy particles of caramelised sugar in the melted chocolate and you will not get a smooth finish.

** Tempered chocolate must be kept at these temperatures while you are working with it.

When you temper chocolate, a room temperature of 21°C with low humidity is ideal, as chocolate contains very little water and tends to absorb it from the atmosphere. Excess humidity can cause an irreversible sugar 'bloom' in the set chocolate; this is when sugar crystals migrate to the surface of the chocolate, dissolve in the water sitting on its surface, and re-crystallise. Cocoa butter 'bloom' looks similar, but it *is* reversible; you just need to melt the chocolate and re-temper it. An easy way to tell if your chocolate has a cocoa butter or sugar 'bloom' is to rub it with your finger – the cocoa butter will melt and the sugar will not.

There are a few ways to temper chocolate – here are the two main techniques we use and refer to in this book.

TABLIER METHOD

Chocolatiers traditionally use the tablier method. It is quick and efficient once you are used to it, works well for large quantities of chocolate (1–5 kg) and the marble or granite slab stays cool and helps the crystals align, unlike metal, which absorbs and retains heat. Once the chocolate is tempered, you can keep working with it for quite a while, heating up a little when it starts to crystallise, and you can temper more chocolate than you need and keep what's left over to re-temper another time.

TOOLS AND EQUIPMENT

Make sure that all your tools and equipment are clean and ready to use. You will need the following (see page 248 for stockists):

— Large stepped palette knife with crooked heel
— Triangle blade
— Scraper
— Marble or granite slab
— Thermometer, preferably digital
— Bain-marie
— Moulds (if using)

1. Melt 1–2kg dark chocolate couverture, broken into small pieces in a large bowl over a bain-marie to 50–55°C. Check that it is completely melted or decrystallised (solid crystals interfere with the tempering process).

2. Pour three-quarters of the melted chocolate on to a clean and dry marble or granite surface. Keep the remaining quarter of chocolate in a small bowl set to one side.

3. Spread the chocolate out into a large circle on the marble slab using the flat edge of the palette knife in your left hand, and with the triangle blade in your right hand push the chocolate from the outside of the circle back into the centre. Each time you make a stroke, scrape the chocolate off the triangle on the edge of the palette knife, held above the centre of the marble. The triangle blade does all the moving, the palette knife stays relatively still. You should now have a smaller circle of chocolate. Spread it thin again into a larger circle with the palette knife, and start pushing the chocolate again with the triangle blade. You will soon begin to feel some resistance as the chocolate thickens, and it should have a silky sheen. This is the sign that the chocolate is cooling and crystals are forming. Regularly test the temperature, and when it reaches 29°C it has cooled enough and should have a satin sheen. It will not be as shiny as it was and it will have thickened to the consistency of clotted cream.

4. Quickly scrape the chocolate back into the empty large bowl. Check the temperature of the untempered quarter of chocolate in the small bowl; if it's warm and still fluid, add some of it to the large bowl of cooled chocolate and stir to combine. If the small bowl is cool to touch, check the temperature (you may need to give it one or two 15–30-second bursts in the microwave to bring it back up to 50°C). The two chocolates mixed in the bowl should have cooled to the correct temperature as recommended on page 227 (i.e. 31–32°C for dark chocolate). Check it is tempered by dipping one side of a small piece of silicone or greaseproof paper in the chocolate. Leave the paper, chocolate side up, on the side at room temperature for a few minutes. If it sets evenly and with no streaking, then the chocolate is tempered.

5. Now the chocolate is ready to be used for moulding, dipping or decorations (see Decorating Chocolate). Your tempered chocolate will not remain stable for long, so you will need to work fast. If it cools, add a little more hot chocolate or use a hair dryer to warm it a little or heat it in the microwave (for just a few seconds) or over a bain-marie to keep the temperature constant. Even professional chocolatiers have days when chocolate refuses to behave, so much patience and practice is needed. Happily you can carry on melting and re-tempering as many times as you like. As long as no water gets into it, it can be decrystallised and recrystallised.

SEEDING METHOD

Often favoured by pastry chefs, this method is useful when you want to make a small quantity of tempered chocolate (20–500g). It involves melting chocolate, then introducing solid tempered chocolate to the melted chocolate to 'seed' the crystals in the liquid chocolat. It is simpler and cleaner than the tablier method.

1. In a large bowl over a bain-marie, melt two-thirds of the chocolate until it is perfectly smooth and fluid, (following the melting part of the temperature guide, see page 227). If you are tempering micro quantities, a small bowl over a mug of boiled water works.

2. Add the remaining third of solid tempered chocolate (it can be a single chunk or chips of chocolate, but it must be at room temperature) to the melted chocolate and stir it vigorously with a rubber spatula. The action of moving the melted chocolate and cooling it with the solid piece/chips mimics the effect of the cool marble in the tablier method.

3. When the chocolate has reached the tempering temperature, all of the chips should be melted. If they have all melted and the chocolate is still too hot, then you need to add some more chips. If using a single chunk, remove what is left of the single chunk of chocolate. You don't need to over-cool it as you are adding the seed. Conduct a paper test (see tablier method) to check it is tempered and use it for dipping or moulding.

MAKING CHABLON

'Chablon' is the technical term for a very thin layer of chocolate that acts as a base for a ganache. It gives chocolates a professional finish, and give them a solid base so that when you dip the ganache in tempered chocolate with a dipping fork, the ganache doesn't sink into the fork and get stuck.

Lightly grease the surface of a flat tray (minumum 20 x 20cm) with a flavourless oil, cover it with clingfilm and, using a paper towel, push out any visible air bubbles from the centre outwards. Using a pastry brush, paint the tempered chocolate on to the clingfilm, taking it to the edges of the tray so that it leaves a margin for your 18 x 18cm stainless steel frame. Place the steel frame on top and leave it to set while you make your ganache.

It is worthwhile going to the extra effort of making a chablon base for the following chocolate recipes, to give them a flawless finish:

Coffee and Lemon Truffles page 32
Olive Oil, Lemon and Basil Truffles page 38
Salted Caramel Truffles page 44
Hazelnut Praline Rochers page 48

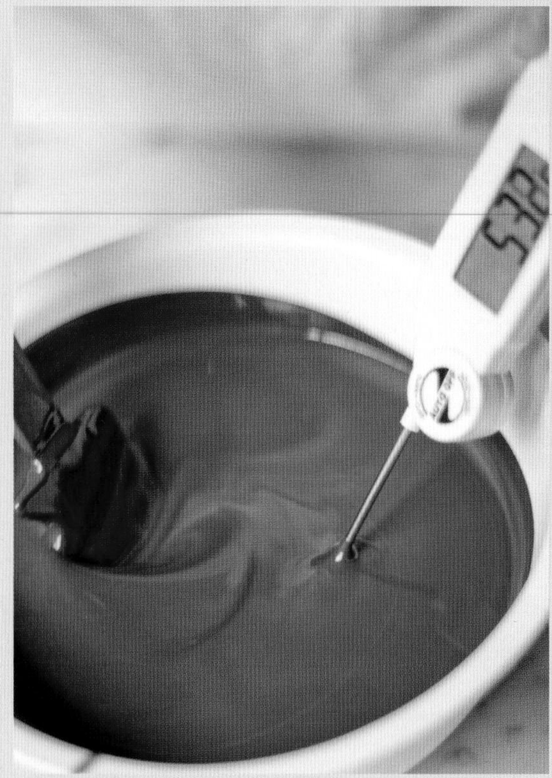

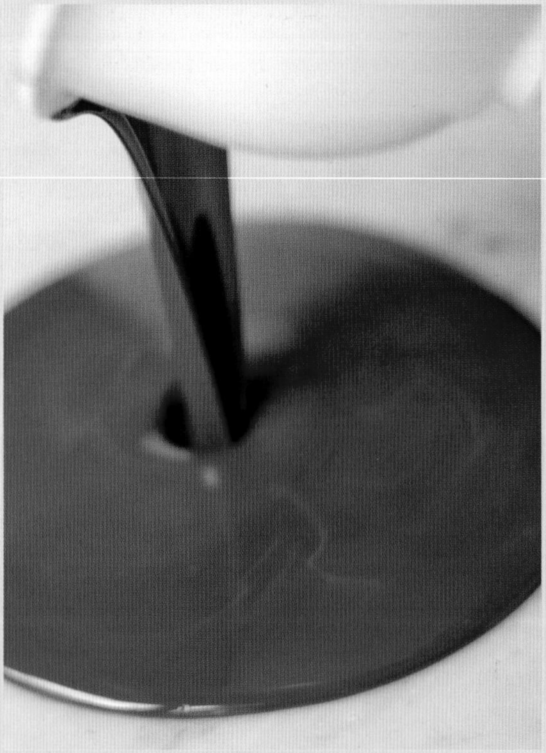

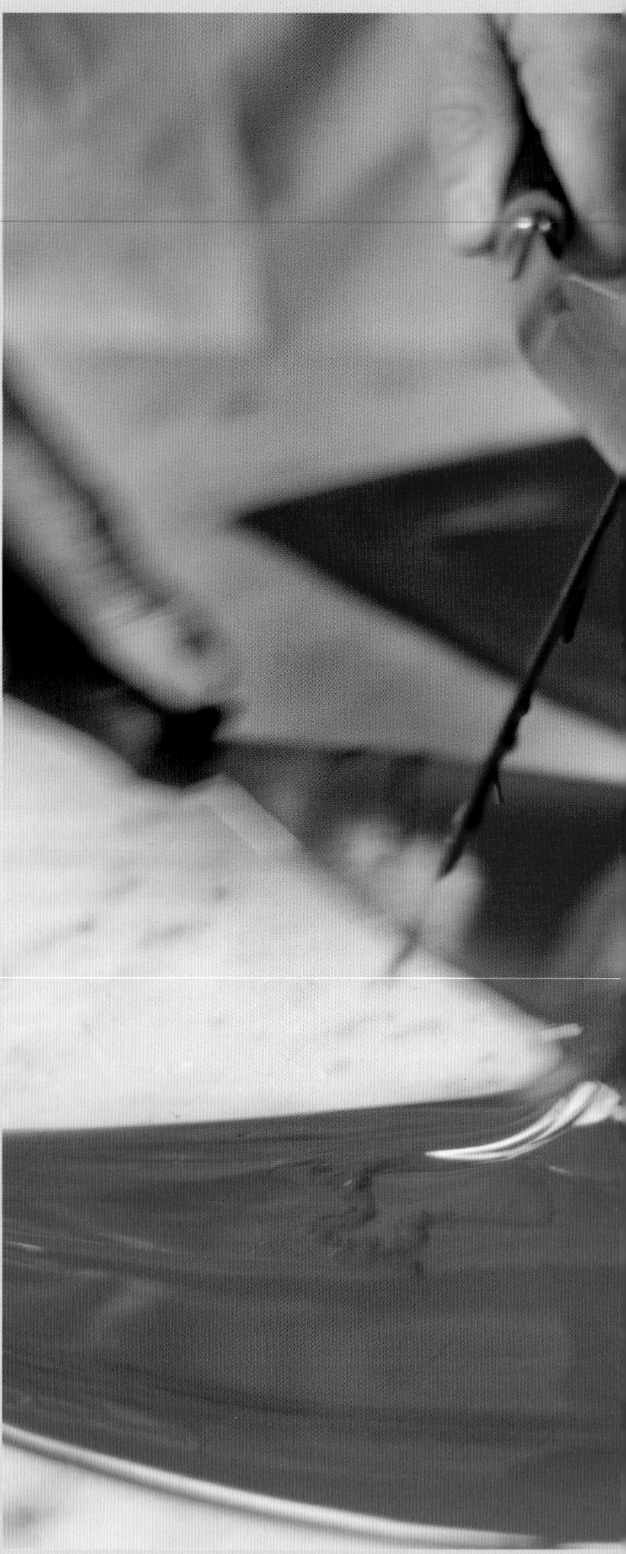

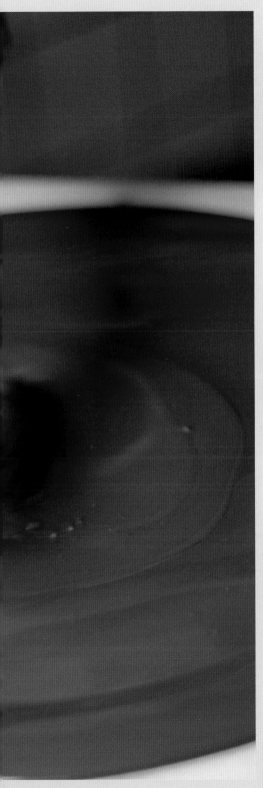

CHOC—OLATE GANA—CHE

Ganache is the foundation of all chocolate truffles.

A ganache is an emulsion, a fragile suspension of two ingredients
that do not naturally mix: fat and liquid. The apocryphal tale is that
chocolate ganache was invented in the 19th century in France or
Switzerland. Imagine the scene: a busy chocolate kitchen, an alpha-male
pastry chef, and a young apprentice who accidentally spills cream into
a bowl of melting chocolate. The chef shouts 'GANACHE!', which
roughly translates as 'idiot'. The resulting silky-smooth emulsion was
wondrous, and the name has stuck to this day. It is a pretty frivolous
story, though I find that most 'eureka' moments come from making
mistakes, and occasionally they can be genius ideas, like this one.

I am certain that the name 'truffle' was adopted as a playful reference
to its striking physical similarity to the *Tuber melanosporum*, or black Per-
igord truffle, so prized in the classic gourmet kitchen. We created
a chocolate truffle with pure truffle essence once, and while it is an
intriguing flavour combination, it's not one of my favourites, as I find
that the musky, earthy notes do not complement cocoa.

Ganache is used to fill chocolate truffles or pralines, or used as a base
or filling for mousses, cakes and desserts. It can be enriched with
additional ingredients such as butter, which also improves its texture
and enhances its taste, and flavourings such as fruits, extracts, spices
and liquors. I love a truffle that melts in the mouth – perfectly made,
very fresh and simple, made with the best chocolate you can get your
hands on.

I like to think of ganache as a metaphor for successful relationships.
It challenges us to find a way to create a perfect union with two separate
entities that do not have a natural affinity for one another. Sometimes it
can go wrong, and the elements split apart. However, with persistence
and goodwill, the two can be brought together again harmoniously.
Making a ganache can be technically tricky, but it needn't be; with a little
guidance, and a bit of practice, it can be truly simple and pleasurable
to make.

You will find all my favourite recipes for chocolate truffles in this
book, but first I want to share with you the fail-safe basic technique
for making the ganache. Keeping the temperature of the mixture
above 35°C throughout ensures success, so always have a probe
thermometer to hand.

1. Set a heatproof bowl over a pan of barely simmering water, making sure that the bottom of the bowl is not touching the water. This water bath is called a bain-marie. Place the chocolate, chopped or broken into small pieces, in the bowl and gently warm it through until melted. Make sure the chocolate does not get too hot, and that no steam gets into the bowl. Set aside.

2. Place the whipped cream in a heavy-based saucepan with liquid glucose or honey and bring it to the boil, then take it off the heat.

3. Stir one-third of the cream into the melted chocolate with a rubber spatula, working from the centre of the bowl outwards. The mixture will start to emulsify. You may think disaster has struck because the mixture thickens dramatically and often splits (the fat and liquid separate). Fear not. After gradually beating the remaining cream into the chocolate, the mixture will become glossy and velvety smooth, and it will not split again.

4. If the ganache recipe contains butter, it must be incorporated at this final stage. Test the temperature of the chocolate, which should not exceed 40°C, then add cubed softened unsalted butter, a little at a time, stirring to incorporate after each addition.

5. Pour the ganache into a frame, tin, tray or box, lined with clingfilm. Leave it to set at room temperature, then chill for a few hours (or overnight) in the fridge, before piping, cutting or rolling and decorating (see page 46).

Refer to the recipe section for actual quantities.

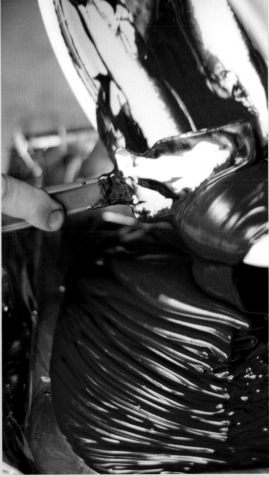

INGRE— DIENTS

CHOCOLATE

The cocoa tree or *Theobroma cacao* is said to have originated deep in the Amazon rainforests in central South America. The cocoa pods grow out of the trunk and branches of the cocoa tree. Inside the pods are rows of slippery white fruit surrounding cocoa seeds. While the fruit is delicious, with a tropical sweet-sour flavour not unlike a lychee, the raw seeds are full of alkaloids and astringent phenolic compounds and are inedible. It is awe-inspiring that someone thought to take this fruit, ferment the seeds, and roast and grind them to make the early forms of rich and highly nutritious chocolate. The first chocolate was not eaten but drunk, by the Toltecs, Mayans and Aztecs, and arrived in Europe via Spain at the end of the 16th century. The beans were not ground into a fine paste and made into bars of chocolate until the age of steam power. Joseph Fry in Bath, England was the first to do this in 1795. Soon after, Rudolf Lindt invented the first conch and Conrad Van Houten, the first cocoa butter press.

There are fundamentally two varieties of bean: the criollo, recognised as the finest bean in the world with the most delicate flavour, and the forastero, which makes up the bulk of the world's production and is not known for its fine flavour but is more robust and heavy yielding. There are also many hybrids, some of which fall into the category of 'fine and flavour' beans, the trinitario from Grenada being the most notable, with a very fine flavour profile and the robust genetics of the forastero. The coffee equivalent would be Arabica and Robusta.

THE JOURNEY FROM COCOA TREE TO BAR

We know that the soil type or terroir, the combination of the land, location, sea breezes, altitude and weather patterns, have a huge part to play in the flavour of wine. The care taken at each stage of wine production affects the final bouquet, and it is exactly the same with cocoa and chocolate, yet how many of us really care about where cocoa comes from or the journey from cocoa tree to bar of chocolate? That journey begins with where it is grown and harvested.

HARVESTING

Cocoa is harvested continually during the cocoa season, which starts in October and continues until April. There are two main harvests, but the fruit ripen at different times, so many diligent cocoa farmers will take the ripe pods only every few days. The cocoa pod is cut from the tree with a special cutting hook, and split open to strip out the cocoa fruit or 'wet cocoa'. The fruit is then fermented, normally very close to where it grows.

FERMENTATION

This stage of chocolate making is poorly understood, particularly by industrial chocolate makers who are often completely divorced from the process; they buy in the fermented and dried beans often without any input at this critical stage. The flavours of cocoa, or polyphenols, develop during the fermentation stage, after it has been harvested. The process is very similar to wine-making. The cocoa bean is surrounded by the white fleshy fruit of the cocoa pod. When I show people fresh cocoa pods, they often mistakenly assume that the white fruit is the cocoa butter (in fact, cocoa butter is extracted from the cocoa bean). The cocoa fruit naturally starts to ferment in the tropical heat, and wild yeasts in the fermentation boxes kick-start the process. Some cocoa growers inoculate the cocoa with yeast cultures to have closer control over this process. The cocoa is fermented for 4–6 days, and as it does so it develops hundreds of flavour components. The chocolate aromas we all love are locked into the beans at this moment, and will be released when the beans are dried and roasted. If cocoa is fermented for too long, lactic acids develop and these can give undesirable cheesy notes. Once the beans are spread out to dry, the fermentation process stops.

DRYING

Drying usually takes place close to where the cocoa grows. The fermented beans are moved to a flat, sunny area: an area of ground covered in concrete, a patch of mud, or purpose-built drawers that can be rolled under cover. The cocoa harvest often coincides with heavy tropical rainfall and if the beans cannot dry quickly enough they become mouldy: a disaster in terms of the beans' flavour. If the cocoa gets damp it's often dried over smoky fires, resulting in smoky or mouldy beans. Inferior beans are sometimes used by chocolate makers, who mask the smoky and mouldy taste with large quantities of sugar and synthetic vanilla (see page 245), but good chocolate makers do not use these beans. In Grenada, where cocoa farming and chocolate making at the Grenada Chocolate Company is challenging conventional wisdom, they have developed a simple and effective 'appropriate technology' solution, harnessing the sun's power to dry the beans. The drying sheds are built with clear corrugated plastic that keeps out air-borne contaminants from animals, birds or insects.

SORTING

Sorting dried cocoa beans is a painstaking process. Large manufacturers with huge factories have expensive machines to sort the beans, but smaller operations do it by hand, removing bad beans that have not dried properly or which have been attacked by insects. If the beans are not adequately hand-sorted, or are sorted by a sub-standard machine, inferior beans will ultimately have a detrimental effect on the flavour of the chocolate. I have tasted chocolate from top chocolate makers tainted with the flavour of mouldy beans.

ROASTING AND WINNOWING

The time and temperature at which beans are roasted are secrets that most chocolate makers do not want to share. The important thing to understand is that the beans are roasted at an even temperature, not too hot and for just the right amount of time to bring out all the nutty aromas without burning the beans. Poor quality beans are often over-roasted deliberately and used to make bitter dark chocolate. After roasting, the beans go through a process of winnowing to remove the husks, leaving the cocoa nibs. The nibs are now ready to be ground.

GRINDING

Grinding refines cocoa nibs into a paste, and eventually into a liquid. Smaller, artisan operations use a melangeur with granite rollers, and large manufacturers use a series of steel rollers, to grind the beans to the required particle size (around 20 microns), which is imperceptible on the tongue. The micron size is really important: at 30 microns you will feel the grains on your tongue, and at 15 the chocolate will be muddy, so it needs to be just right. These days many micro chocolate makers are grinding their own beans with smaller *gringeurs*, a version of the melangeur, to make 10–20kg batches of chocolate.

CONCHING

Conching releases many of the acidic volatile components that help create complex flavours when fermentation takes place, creating a chocolate with finesse and a deep, smooth and mellow flavour profile. It can take hours or days, depending on the equipment used. In Grenada, the conch is a large drum that looks a bit like a giant washing machine. The liquid chocolate is turned around to allow the air to reach every particle. The process allows the acidic volatile components to evaporate into the air, which is vented out of the machine. Generally, the finer the flavour desired, the longer the conch. Fine chocolate stands out because it is softer and smoother than industrial chocolate, which often leaves the teeth on edge because of the residual acidity trapped in the beans.

TEMPERING

After conching, the melted chocolate is transferred to tempering tanks, where it is agitated and cooled so that the complex crystallisation process can take place. This is what gives chocolate its wonderful shine, crisp snap and melt-in-the-mouth qualities. Now the chocolate can be moulded into tablets, to be eaten in that form, or into buttons to be used to make into other things.

BUYING GOOD CHOCOLATE

These days it is much easier to find good quality chocolate for cooking; even the lovely Grenada Chocolate Company chocolate can be found in Whole Foods, in our shops, on our website, in Waitrose and at other specialist retailers. For that reason, I am using it as our default chocolate in this book, though of course you can substitute it for another good quality chocolate. I will now attempt to lead you through the minefield of how to choose the best chocolate.

At Rococo we use our chocolate from Grenada as well as Valrhona couvertures and organic chocolates in our blends. Most people accept that 70% cocoa solids is a good thing, and an indicator of quality. I rue the day I declared, in the early 90s when I was setting up The Chocolate Society, that it was the benchmark for fine chocolate. Actually at that time it was pretty much true, though the big manufacturers quickly caught on to it, so the '70% chocolate myth' is now ubiquitous. I would like to quickly de-bunk this one – it's just like saying 'I choose my wine by the volume of alcohol on the label – the higher, the better'. From 55% upwards, you can find exceptional chocolate and of course there are lots of great chocolates with 70% cocoa or more, but there are also lots of unpleasant ones with bitter burnt notes, added cocoa powder, and a reluctance to melt or behave in the way we might want it to, especially when baking or making chocolates. Take the percentage with a pinch of salt and check out the ingredients; don't buy it if it is made with artificial vanillin or any fats other than cocoa butter. If the label mentions where the cocoa is from, or the type of cocoa bean used, it will probably be a better chocolate.

Milk chocolate is made by adding milk solids to dark chocolate. Some chocolate manufacturers, particularly in the USA and UK, add milk 'crumb' which is slightly fermented and gives the chocolate a characteristic farmyard flavour, while in continental Europe a sweeter powdered milk is added, giving the chocolate a creamy caramel flavour. Most people love the mass-produced milk chocolate that they were given as children, however well developed their critical faculties have become, as it offers a moment of sensual transportation to childhood.

White chocolate is very much frowned upon by chocolate purists, who claim it is not chocolate at all. Technically they are correct, if you define chocolate by its dry cocoa content, rather than by its cocoa butter content. Good quality white chocolate is made with pure cocoa butter, milk solids, sugar and vanilla, and it provides a perfect foil to sharp fruity flavours. One of my personal favourites is the Rococo Lemon and Violet, a white chocolate ganache covered in milk chocolate.

COCOA BUTTER AND COUVERTURE CHOCOLATE

Extracting cocoa butter from cocoa beans is not an easy process. The cocoa beans are roasted, and the nibs are ground into cocoa liquor. This liquor is then poured into a custom-made cocoa butter press to extract the cocoa butter, leaving behind the dry cocoa cake. The Grenada Chocolate Company have invented a unique micro process, using small presses that exert two tonnes of weight per square inch to squeeze the butter out of the cocoa mass. The residual cocoa cakes are ground into Smilo cocoa tea, as it is known on the island – or unsweetened drinking chocolate to the rest of us.

One word that chocolatiers often use is 'viscosity', which describes fluidity or lack of fluidity; the act of a substance becoming thick and sticky due to friction. For a chocolatier, the perfect chocolate has added cocoa butter, which improves the fluidity of the chocolate when it melts, giving a wonderful soft mouth feel, and helps release the complex flavour or phenolic profile of the cocoa used. This high cocoa butter chocolate is called couverture, and chocolatiers like to use it because it behaves in a predictable way, and after tempering it re-crystallises to form beautifully shiny, crisp chocolate. Any fine eating chocolate should be, by definition, couverture.

HOW TO TASTE CHOCOLATE

When tasting chocolate all the senses are involved, from listening to the crack when a piece of perfectly tempered chocolate is snapped to looking at it to see the beautiful shine (or lack of), smelling it to see if you can discern good or bad aromas. Generally, good ones are deeply fruity chocolate notes and natural vanilla – the more complex flavours open up once the chocolate is on the palette. Often you can spot bad notes, burnt elements, rubber, petrol, and the injudicious use of artificial vanillins.

The touch of the chocolate and speed of melt on the tongue are clues to the purity of the chocolate; if it's slow to melt or chalky in the mouth, it may be a sign of cheaper and less desirable fats being substituted in place of cocoa butter. When you allow chocolate to melt very slowly in your mouth, try not to chew to speed up the process; you will find the complex, volatile aromas rising into the nose where we can detect hundreds of different flavour components. It is noticeable when you have a cold that your sense of taste is significantly diminished – you can try a simple test of just holding your nose closed to see how it affects the flavour of the chocolate.

It takes a brave chocolate maker to eschew vanilla and allow the beans to speak for themselves. We have just had a special small edition bar – the Gru Grococo – made from one harvest of beans grown on our small farm by our partner, the Grenada Chocolate Company. It is a pure Trinitario bean, 66% cocoa solids, with added cocoa butter and no vanilla, shipped under sail by the Fair Transport brigantine *Tres Hombres* across the Atlantic, and aged in oak during the voyage and a zero carbon footprint to boot. I believe this is a first, certainly this century!

CREAM

We get through an awful lot of cream at Rococo. It is the mainstay of our fresh ganaches and gives the chocolates a wonderfully rich texture. Cream has a remarkable consistency, possessing the perfect balance of solidity and fluidity. Ethereal yet tenacious, it can be tart, sweet, fresh or cool, and it lingers luxuriously in the mouth without leaving any greasy particles or cloying the palette. This mouthfeel is the result of 'crowding' fat globules that are far too small to detect on the tongue. In addition to its great texture, cream has distinctive aroma notes (lactones) from molecules that are also found in coconut and peaches.

From a chocolate-making and scientific perspective, it is important to understand that cream is a natural emulsion of water and fat. It is the rich fatty part of milk, which floats to the top in full cream milk. As well as fat, it offers proteins and emulsifying molecules (it is an emulsion of butterfat and water) that can help stabilise other more fragile emulsions such as ganache, where the cream acts as the water and the chocolate as the fat. One similar emulsion is mayonnaise, an emulsion of egg yolk and oil.

There are many schools of thought on the perfect way to mix cream into chocolate – whether it should be boiled first, gently heated or used cold – and all of them have their advocates, but this is not something we need to get too hung up about in domestic production.

Most cream used in chocolate-making and baking is pasteurised. We use Normandy whipping cream in all our chocolates. Using the same cream in all our recipes brings consistency and means we know how long they will keep.

FAT CONTENT

Because of the high proportion of fat to proteins, cream is less likely to curdle than milk, and can be inflated (whipped). For cream to whip to peaks, it needs a minimum fat content of 30%. The higher the fat content of the cream, the quicker it will thicken, and it will have a denser, less voluminous texture. The whipping cream we use has a fat content of 35–38%. Lighter creams such as 'légère', 'fleurette' or 'épaisse' can be used, though I would not recommend them, as they are less stable when heated.

THIS CHART ILLUSTRATES THE FAT CONTENT IN DIFFERENT KINDS OF CREAM.

Fat content, as a percentage %	
UK	
Single cream	18
Whipping	35–38
Double	48
Clotted	55
France	
Crème fleurette	30–40
Crème fraîche	30–40
Crème légère	12–30
Crème épaisse	40+
USA	
Light cream	20
Light whipping cream	30–36
Whipping cream	35+
Heavy cream	38+

HOW TO WHIP CREAM

Physical agitation miraculously transforms this delicious but unstable liquid into a shapeable solid. The process of whipping captures air bubbles in the butterfat. If the cream gets warm, the bubbles will collapse, so for best results start with everything as cold as possible (around 4°C), including the cream. If your kitchen is very warm, chill your bowl and whisk. Use an electric hand whisk or free-standing electric mixer. Whip the cream slowly at first (this will encourage it to capture more air bubbles), increasing the speed to medium and whipping until it reaches soft peak stage, which is ideal for mousses, or stiff peak stage, ideal for piping or spooning. If you whip the cream for too long, it will become stiff and ultimately turn to butter and buttermilk.

BUTTER

'Coagulated sunlight…heaped up like gilded gravel in the bowl.'

Irish poet, Seamus Heaney,
describing butter in
Churning Day

Butter has been much maligned in recent decades.
Now it is finally regaining its reputation as a natural
and nutritious fat that has been enjoyed for centuries.

BUTTER IN BAKING

I always choose butter when I make cakes and pastry
(I have an aversion to margarine). Much of the flavour
and pleasure in baking comes from the butter, which
contributes up to a third of the total weight of the mixture.
It is the traditional fat chosen by pastry chefs, who value
its flavour and richness as much as its texture. By beating
sugar and butter together to incorporate air bubbles the
mixture reaches a fluffy consistency, and lightens the
texture of the finished cake. Butter, as a solid fat, retains
these air bubbles more efficiently. I've used an unsalted
or lightly salted French butter for all the baking recipes
in this book. Speciality professional baker's butter, made
predominantly in France and sometimes referred to as 'dry'
(cultured) butter, has a higher fat content and less water
than standard butter, which can be an advantage when
making pastry.

BUTTER IN CHOCOLATE MAKING

The butter in chocolate locks in all the delicate flavours
and adds freshness in the mouth. Our chocolatier likes
to use butter with 84% fat content, which has a higher
melting point. This helps preserve delicate flavours in the
chocolate because it absorbs them during the chocolate-
making process and releases them as it melts in the mouth
during tasting (the melting point of butter is around body
temperature). Some fats, like lard, melt above body temperature and leave a fatty layer in the mouth, which is not
desirable. In chocolate making, all recipes need an overall
fat content of 10–15%, which can come from the butter or
the cream. Chocolatiers often choose butter with a higher
fat content, and consequently less water, to give more
stability to their ganaches.

There is an overwhelming choice of butter in the shops,
though most brands can be divided into two types, both
of which we use to make our chocolates.

Cultured cream butter is common unsalted butter, consumed
widely in Europe, made from pasteurised raw cream,
fermented over several days by the bacterial action of added
lactic acids. It has some acidity, a good aroma and a full and
rich flavour, with a standard fat content of 80%.

Sweet cream butter is made by churning pasteurised fresh
cream in a chilled environment. This is the most common
kind of butter in the UK and USA and it is often salted.
It has a standard fat content of at least 80%.

HOW TO KEEP AND STORE BUTTER

Good quality butter is quite resilient and keeps well
for a few days at room temperature. This makes it perfect
for spreading on your toast in the morning; there's nothing
more irritating than trying to spread hard butter straight
from the fridge. Shopbought *spreadable* butters have oil
added, and we don't recommend their use in baking. Most
of our recipes suggest using butter at room temperature. It
must be said, however, that its delicate flavour is susceptible
to strong aromas, and prolonged exposure to air and light
will hasten deterioration and eventually cause the butter
to become rancid. Therefore, weigh the amount you need
for the recipe a couple of hours in advance and leave it out
to reach room temperature before you use it. Butter, well
wrapped, can be kept in the fridge for at least 1 month,
and can also be frozen.

Butter is such a joy to make with children. Just take a pot
of double cream and beat it until golden balls of butter
start to form on the surface and cling together, leaving
rich buttermilk behind that you can use to make the most
delicious scones.

VANILLA

One of the most controversial subjects in the world of chocolate is vanilla. Almost certainly one of the most universally popular flavours to mankind, it seems that even a breastfed baby can distinguish the flavour of vanilla when their mother has eaten it.

Vanilla comes from the pod fruit of the orchid *planifolia* (*V. fragrens*) and is indigenous to Mexico. First brought to Europe at the time of the Spanish Conquest in the early 16th century, the plant was studied by botanists for over two hundred years before they worked out how pollination takes place in the natural environment. Charles Darwin was one of those who spent many hours pondering 'what strange creatures these orchids are'. The Belgian botanist, Charles Morren, finally cracked the technique of pollination in the 19th century, using a small paintbrush to hand-pollinate the first European Orchid. From Europe, the orchids were taken to Madagascar and Réunion, where they now flourish. We use Ndali vanilla from Uganda, which is the first Fairtrade vanilla in the world.

Natural vanilla is the second most expensive flavouring in the world after saffron, and has over 200 volatile flavour components. Yet 97% of vanilla used commercially as a flavouring or fragrance is synthetic. As vanilla is extremely difficult to cultivate and costly, and demand far exceeds availability, the flavour is artificially produced. Synthetic vanillin is made on an industrial scale in laboratories by growing the crystals extracted from pine. This artificial flavouring lacks the flavour complexity of natural vanilla and has been a source of great concern to many chocolate activists, though I am happy to say that the fine chocolate industry is taking action, and it is rare to find artificial vanillin on the list of ingredients in good quality chocolate. The name vanillin is extremely confusing, as vanillin crystals form naturally on vanilla pods when they are cured, and are naturally present in wood (this explains why many barrel-aged wines have vanilla notes). Used judiciously, real vanilla is a bit like salt or sugar, a seasoning that will enhance a recipe.

The vanilla bean looks very much like a runner bean when it is on the orchid, about 15 cm long, round, and green in colour. The beans are gathered, steamed or boiled, exposed to the heat of the sun to start the curing process, wrapped up to 'sweat', then dried and aged. It takes weeks and sometimes months to do this, and much hard work, and in this time the complex and rich flavour components develop. The most prized and expensive vanilla pods have a frosting of naturally occurring vanillin crystals on the outside. Vanilla has properties that naturally inhibit the action of microbes, so it acts as a preservative. It is also the most effective antidote to mouldy flavours, hence the copious amounts of artificial vanillin in cheap chocolate, where it is used to disguise the putrid notes of badly fermented cocoa beans. Only the very bravest of chocolate makers does not add vanilla when grinding the cocoa beans. You need to be supremely confident in the quality of the cocoa beans to do this. Vanilla can hide a multitude of sins. We are very proud of our new single-estate Gru Grococo made without vanilla. It's an extremely elegant and fruity chocolate, the pedigree of the cocoa shining out.

SUGAR

Our brains are hard-wired to love sweet things. Sugar, pure unadulterated sweetness, is highly addictive. The more sugar you eat, the deeper the neural pathways etch themselves into your brain, as with any substance that is habit-forming, such as fat and salt. I was shocked when an Italian ice-cream machine manufacturer told me that he was asked by a large multinational fast-food chain how much salt they could add to a slush drink in order to make it particularly addictive, and the consumer very thirsty. There are some dark forces at work, and although it's great to know exactly what is added to our food, the best way to avoid these evils is to make it ourselves using fresh ingredients.

In its pure white incarnation, refined sugar is a relative newcomer, arriving in Europe in the 16th century. Going back to the beginnings of time, our earliest experience of sweetness would have come as mother's milk. Then, for millions of years, it was honey and the natural sugars in fruit. Cane sugar, in its refined state, was for a long time very expensive and consumed in tiny quantities. These days most refined sugar is made from beet and the group of sugar alcohols that have been around since the 1970s, all of which are very cheap to produce.

There is plenty of evidence linking epidemic obesity, raised LDL cholesterol levels and diabetes to high fructose corn syrup (HFCS), which is ubiquitous in the USA and is found in almost all processed foods, such as bread, cereals, yoghurt, processed meats and soups. We are bombarded with refined sugar at every turn, be it the 20 spoonfuls in a can of fizzy drink or the sweeteners hidden in processed foods: it's hard to avoid. Industrial confectionery is full of it, and though the occasional bite of something sweet is harmless enough, it's good to be in control of how we consume sugar. Of course, we give you dispensation to eat one of our marshmallows (see page 68) as a bit of treat in your carefully balanced diet!

There is a bewildering array of sugars and sweeteners out there. These are the sugars most often used in chocolate making, which we use for different purposes.

Granulated sugar:
This is the best sugar for making syrups and caramels. It has the largest crystals but is susceptible to crystallisation.
Caster sugar (including golden):
Works best in cake recipes where you are creaming the sugar with butter.
Brown sugars:
We use brown sugar when we want to add flavour or texture to the finished recipe, eg. Chocolate Crunch Eclairs (see page 138).
Icing sugar:
Powdered sugar dissolves well and gives the finished recipe no texture, so it is normally used in products that aren't going to be cooked.
Liquid glucose:
Helps to stop crystallisation in cooked sugar and improves the texture in ganaches.
Honey:
Gives a characteristic flavour and can be used instead of glucose.

Different sugars have different amounts of sweetness. The scale of sweetness below puts sucrose (white sugar) at 100 and glucose 70–80, whereas fructose is 140, making it much sweeter than sugar.

Relative Sweetness Scale: Sucrose = 100	
Compound	**Rating**
Fructose	140
High Fructose Corn Syrup (HFCS)	120–160
Sucrose	100
Glucose	70–80
Galactose	35
Maltose	30–50
Lactose	20

Source:
http://chemwiki.ucdavis.edu

EGGS

Eggs are perfect food parcels. They contain protein, fat and vitamins – just what is needed to nourish a baby chick, or a human. The yolk contains all the fats, fatty acids, vitamins, minerals and most of the protein. The white consists of 90% water and 10% protein, with only traces of the nutritious elements in the yolk. Although the yolks contain a small amount of cholesterol, it is not like saturated fat that can raise cholesterol levels, so you can eat eggs as a guilt-free part of your balanced diet.

It is not easy to make a cake without eggs and we use plenty of them in this book. Eggs form the base of most chocolate mousses, too. Pastry chefs and chocolatiers like precision when baking and making mousses, and often measure egg whites and yolks in grammes. We have translated these gramme measurements into standard units of medium or large eggs, using the chart below, to make the recipes more user friendly.

Very Large	73g +over	Size 0/1
Large	63–73g	Size 1/2/3
Medium	53–63g	Size 3/4/5
Small	53g + under	Size 5/6/7

FRESHNESS

Old eggs are better for boiling, because they are easier to peel (anyone who has ever tried to peel a fresh quails egg will testify to this), but we like to use the freshest eggs we can get our hands on for baking. My mother tells me hat when she bought eggs from the itinerant egg man in Tehran she would take a bucket of water to test their fresh-ness. The freshest would sink to the bottom and rotten ones float to the surface (due to the increase in sulphurous gases inside the shell). This technique still holds true and it's a good test if you are ever in doubt about the freshness of an egg, though these days most have a date stamp.

HOW TO STORE

Store eggs in the fridge, but let them come to room tem-perature before using them in baking. Ingredients mix together better if they are all the same temperature.

When you need only egg whites, you may find it convenient to buy pasteurised egg whites in a carton, available from well-stocked delis and supermarkets. Egg whites freeze well. The freezing helps to break down the protein – when you whisk eggs, you are unfolding the proteins so that you can get them to stick to each other, making them easier to whisk. You cannot freeze egg yolks, however, without mixing them with salt, sugar or acid to stop the proteins from sticking together.

TIPS

Whisking egg whites

— Use a spotlessly clean bowl, and make sure the whisk is clean, too. Copper and silver bowls block sulphur reactions between proteins and help create a more stable froth. Glass and metal bowls work well, too, though plastic is harder to get spotlessly clean as it is porous.

— Be careful not to let any egg yolk get into the whites, as the fat will stop the eggs from foaming.

— Once your egg whites are whisked, fold them into the cake mixture gently with a large metal spoon, to avoid losing any of the volume.

Making custards and pastry cream

— Add the sugar to the yolks a couple of hours before you need them, or as soon as you weigh them out. This will increase their tolerance to heat, thus decreasing the likelihood of your custard turning into scrambled egg. The sugar molecules dilute the proteins in the egg yolk and raise the cooking temperature, sometimes referred to as 'burning' the yolks.

If you are keen to find out more about the science of cooking with eggs, refer to Harold McGee's *On Food & Cooking* (Hodder & Stoughton, 2004).

STOCKISTS

These days we can source all kinds of specialist equipment and ingredients from the comfort of our homes on the internet, infinitely preferable to roaming around town and so often leaving empty-handed and frustrated. John Lewis, Divertimenti and Amazon have a great range of cookware online, and you can find good quality chocolate in most high-end supermarkets. Specific couvertures can be found in our shops and online at www.rococochocolate.com, and for all the weird and wonderful ingredients and equipment we use in chocolate making, here is a list of trusted suppliers.

— Freeze-dried fruits: raspberry, passion fruit, yoghurt, strawberry, and blackcurrant
— Valrhona chocolate (Caramelia and Ivoire are the most popular) in bags of buttons or chunks
— Valrhona unsweetened cocoa powder and Grenada Chocolate Co. organic cocoa powder
— Grenada Chocolate Co. bars
— Rococo Artisan bars
— Cocoa nibs
— Cocoa butter
— Popping candy
— Argent assortment dragées
— Stainless steel 18 x 18 cm frame for ganache
  www.rococochocolates.com

— Polystyrene cones (used to make the Choc-en-bouche on page 140)
  www.craftmill.co.uk or cake decorating shops

— Bulk frozen fruit purées (1kg minimum)
— Bulk Valrhona chocolate, Gianduja and ready-made praline pastes, Normandy cream, butter, nuts and oils
  www.classicfinefoods.co.uk

— Chocolate-making equipment, bulk freeze-dried fruits, coloured cocoa butter, chocolate, chocolate dipping forks, polycarbonate moulds and plastic moulds
  www.homechocolatefactory.com

— Bespoke chocolate moulds
  www.chocolatetrays.co.uk

— Bulk Grenada Chocolate Co. couverture
  www.hbingredients.co.uk

— Dried barberries, dried Persian limes, rose petals, and pomegranate molasses
  www.foratasteofpersia.co.uk (Persepolis)

— Edible gold leaf
— Green barley grass powder
— Egg top cutter
— Silicone moulds, bakeware and probe thermometers
  www.amazon.co.uk

— Tabletop tempering machine
  www.chocolatier-electro.com

— Cocoa butter transfer sheets
  www.squires-shop.com and **Keylink** (below)

— Chocolate cups
— Gianduja 'Noisette'
— Crêpes dentelles
— Sugared mint pieces
— Coloured cocoa butters
  www.keylink.org

— Thermomix
  www.thermomix.com

— Disposable piping bags and a set of nozzles
  Any major supermarket or cookware supplier

INDEX

253

DOUG BROWNE
CHOCOLATE ACTIVIST
1966–2008

ACKNOWL— EDGEMENTS

Firstly to all the Rococo family, past and present, especially Barry Johnson, who has worked tirelessly on this book, and to all our customers who have supported us over the years.

To James Booth, all the Coady, Booth and Roden families, especially to Cesar and Claudia. To Millie, for helping to bake all those cakes, and to my dear friends who helped to eat them and gave their honest feedback.

Leigh Jones, for his creativity, amazing sense of fun, and role as midwife to this book as it emerged into the world. James Murphy, for his fabulous photography, Kris Kirkham his able assistant, and Debbie Major who worked like a demon organising, shopping, styling and prepping. Amanda Harris, who commissioned this book, for her vision, clarity, and quiet support. Laura Nickoll, for her huge patience and scrupulous editing. Lucie Stericker and everyone at Orion and my agent, Michael Alcock.

In no particular order, all my colleagues in the world of chocolate, especially the Academy of Chocolate, Laurent Couchaux and Luke Frost, Cristina White da Cruz, The Gentleman Baker, the Percival family, Vanessa Kimble, Cesar Roden, Claudia Roden, Lulu Sturdy, Charlie Boxer, Harold McGee, Mark Prizeman, Tom Assheton of Tomtom cigars, Jane Etherton of Thermomix, Michael Davenport of Dar Interiors, Wendy Hartland, Shadel Nyack-Compton, Tom Dixon, André Dubreuil, Mark Brazier-Jones, Sarah Pinto, Robert Mantho, Sophie and Michael Coe, Kate Griffiths-Lambeth & bees, Emily Readett-Bayley, and last but not least, my personal trainer Deborah Riley.

255

First published in Great Britain in 2012
by Weidenfeld & Nicolson, an imprint of
the Orion Publishing Group Ltd
Orion House, 5 Upper St. Martin's Lane,
London, WC2H 9EA

1 3 5 7 9 10 8 6 4 2

A CIP catalogue record for this book is available
from the British Library.

ISBN: 978 0 297 86519 3

Weidenfeld & Nicolson
The Orion Publishing Group
Orion House
5 Upper St Martin's Lane
London WC2H 9EA

An Hachette UK Company

Rococo Prof du Choc: Barry Johnson
Art Direction and Design: www.stazikerjones.co.uk
Editor: Laura Nickoll
Recipe consultant and food stylist: Debbie Major
Photographer: James Murphy
Photographer's assistant: Kris Kirkham
Props stylist: Giuliana Casarotti
Proofreader: Caroline Curtis
Indexer: Elise See Tai

Printed and bound in China

Photograph on page 17 copyright (c) *The Sunday
Times Magazine* / NI Syndication

The Orion Publishing Group's policy is to use
papers that are natural, renewable and recyclable
products and made from wood grown in sustainable
forests. The logging and manufacturing processes
are expected to conform to the environmental
regulations of the country of origin.

www.orionbooks.co.uk

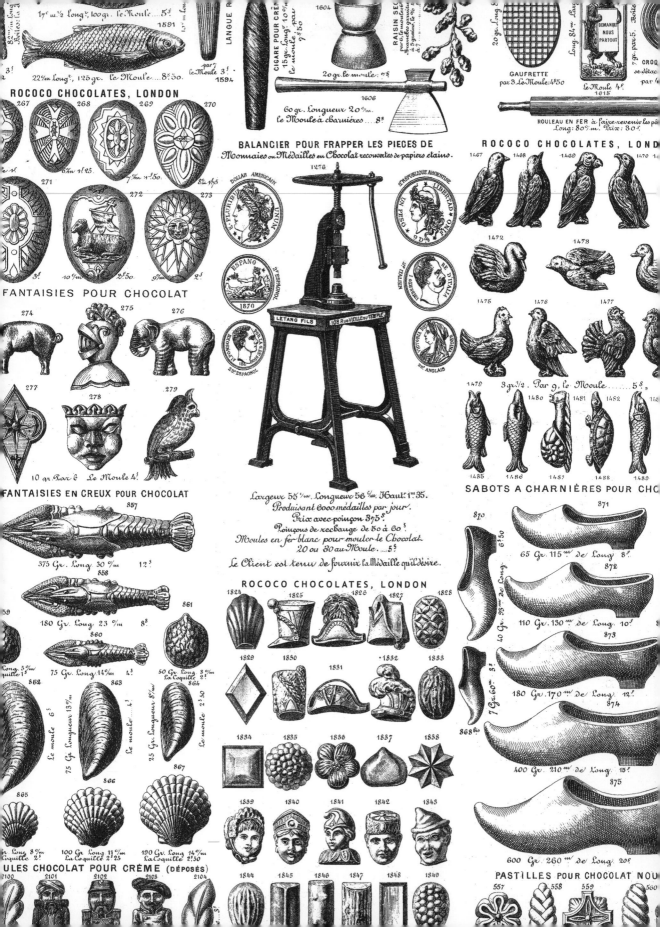

ROCOCO CHOCOLATES, LONDON

BALANCIER POUR FRAPPER LES PIÈCES DE
Monnaies ou Médailles en Chocolat recouvertes de papiers étains.

FANTAISIES POUR CHOCOLAT

FANTAISIES EN CREUX POUR CHOCOLAT

ROCOCO CHOCOLATES, LONDON

ROCOCO CHOCOLATES, LOND

SABOTS A CHARNIÈRES POUR CHO

ULES CHOCOLAT POUR CRÈME (DÉPOSÉS)

PASTILLES POUR CHOCOLAT NOU